"*The Idler's Glossary* condenses so many ideas into its unassuming form that it may well be explosive if exposed to direct sunlight. Several generations of aspiring liggers, cadgers, dossers, and goldbrickers will derive inspiration, intellectual sustenance, and suggestions for further reading from its pages, and Joshua Glenn should be prepared to find himself henceforth very unpopular with Calvinists and timekeepers everywhere."

—Luc Sante is the author of *Low Life*, *Evidence*, *The Factory of Facts*, and, most recently, *Kill All Your Darlings: Pieces 1990–2005*.

"The *Idler's Glossary* is wonderful! I opened it, set it over my eyes and took a delightful two-hour nap. Thank you so much."

—Mark Frauenfelder, founder of BoingBoing.net

The IDLER'S GLOSSARY

The
IDLER'S
GLOSSARY

BY
JOSHUA GLENN
& MARK KINGWELL

DESIGNED + DECORATED BY SETH

BIBLIOASIS

2008

SETH

FIRST EDITION

Library and Archives Canada Cataloguing in Publication

Glenn, Joshua, 1967-
    The idler's glossary / Joshua Glenn and Mark Kingwell ;
illustrator, Seth.

ISBN 10: 1-897231-46-6
ISBN 13: 978-1-897231-46-3

    1. Work—Philosophy—Terminology. 2. Work—Social
aspects—Terminology. 3. Work—Philosophy—Humor.
4. Work—Social aspects—Humor. I. Kingwell, Mark, 1963-
II. Title.

BF485.G58 2008   306.3′6   C2008-904362-6

Edited by Daniel Wells.

PRINTED AND BOUND IN USA

INTRODUCTION

IDLING TOWARD HEAVEN:

The Last Defence
You Will Ever Need

MARK KINGWELL

"*People* of experience maintain that it's very sensible to start from a principle," Søren Kierkegaard writes rather near the middle of his *Either/Or: A Fragment of Life* (1843). "I grant them that and start with the principle that all men are boring." As first principles go that is a sound choice, though often misunderstood by those to whom it most applies.

For example, a frustrated husband in a Kingsley Amis novel relates to a friend that his wife is boring as well as ugly: "[M]y wife accuses me of thinking her boring. It doesn't seem to have occurred to her that this might be because she's boring. . . . To her mind, her being boring is a thing I do." This being a remarkably common misconception, it is worth clarifying, first, that someone's being boring is a thing they do, not you; but also that *in practice* someone's being boring generates a dyadic relation, consisting of the boring being borne by the bored. At no point is it something that latter does.

Alas, the causes of boredom are not limited to the conversation of other people, whether men in general or wives in particular. No, it is a sad truth of this life that one may be bored all by oneself. "Life, friends, is boring," John Berryman averred in a poem. "We must not say so." The reason, the poet tells us, was provided by his mother:

(repeatedly) "Ever to confess you're bored means you have no

Inner Resources." I conclude now I have no inner resources, because I am heavy bored.
Peoples bore me,
literature bores me, especially great literature
[. . .]

Let us agree that life can be boring. Let us do so as forcefully as possible – but not as a complaint, instead as a point of departure. For there is no more certain cause of boredom's continuance than the lifelong flight from its presence, the constant injunction that finding oneself bored is, in some unspecified sense, a moral failure. It is, rather, a deep insight. Human life, says Schopenhauer in *The World as Will and Representation* (1819), "swings like a pendulum to and fro between pain and boredom, and these two are in fact its ultimate constituents." Boredom is "anything but an evil to be thought of lightly: ultimately it depicts the countenance of real despair."

Contrary to received wisdom, there is no escape from this dismal condition via further stimulation of desire – the error of all advertising and most culture. We do not gain insight into our human condition of desire's limit by taking another route to get there, nor by more and more secure satisfaction of existing desires. (If life were a utopia where "pigeons flew about ready roasted," Schopenhauer writes elsewhere, "people would die of boredom or else hang themselves.") Boredom is desire stalled, the "paradoxical wish for a desire" as Adam Phillips has phrased it; the stall is a signal that something has gone wrong with desire, perhaps something big that we need to confront but which under current conditions we cannot. There can be no insight into boredom, and so no respite to be had from its presumed ravages, simply by exciting a new desire to replace the absent one. Desire itself is what must be queried, and that can only be done by moving *inside* desire itself, asking what desire fundamentally is about.

And so enter idling. The relation between boredom and idling suffuses and pervades the aphoristic wisdom contained in the following pages, and reveals the depth of idling's significance to human life. "Idleness as such is by no means a root of evil," Kierkegaard continues in the same section of his work; "quite the contrary, it is a truly divine way of life so long as one is not bored." This is a key qualification, first because it implies that any identification of idling with boredom is an error of categories; but also, second, because it suggests that one value of idling *properly undertaken* is that it offers an investigation of, possibly even a cure to, boredom. "The Latin proverb, *otium est pulvinar diaboli*, is perfectly correct," Kierkegaard adds, "but when one isn't bored the devil gets no time to lay his head on that pillow." Idleness is only the devil's pillow, and idle hands the devil's work – to add the more familiar cognate proverb – when idleness is misunderstood.

* * *

Considering how much time humans have devoted to goofing off, that is unfortunately often. The work-ethic condemnation of idleness as unproductive is familiar; it is rooted in the even older notion that morose idleness is sinful, an insult to God's grace. The shared idea in both secular and religious versions of the condemnation is that if one is not engaged in some useful occupation – if one is not working for gain of some sort, whether money or status or progress in the soul's journey –

then one is committing a kind of failure: to self, to community, to supreme being, or to all three. The presuppositions of this view have been comprehensively dismantled by many philosophers, including Bertrand Russell in his short book *In Praise of Idleness* (1932). Russell extended and by his lights redeemed the merely aesthetic arguments in favour of idleness, the sort of thing familiar from a value-reversing Oscar Wilde *aperçu*, by noting just how unfulfilling and stupid most work actually is. What, after all, is work?

"Work is of two kinds," Russell notes: "first, altering the position of matter at or near the earth's surface relatively to other such matter; second, telling other people to do so. The first kind is unpleasant and ill paid; the second is pleasant and highly paid. The second kind is capable of indefinite extension: there are not only those who give orders, but those who give advice as to what orders should be given. Usually two opposite kinds of advice are given simultaneously by two organized bodies of men; this is called politics. The skill required for this kind of work is not knowledge of the subjects as to which advice is given, but knowledge of the art of persuasive speaking and writing, i.e. of advertising." Not only is the work ethic's disdain of idleness judgmental, it is dunderheaded and pernicious: the scale of value in play is based on a thick layer of mutually reinforcing philosophical errors and arrangements of power.

Fine. The trouble is that such redemption of idleness against the claims of work actually confuses the central issue, making idleness a category inextricable from work in the form of negation. In our tribe's jargon, this is known as dialectical assimilation. If idleness is understood as not-working – as distinct from not working because engaged in doing other things – it remains conceptually beholden to work as that which it is not. Not-working = *failing* to work. Hence the importance of the idler/slacker distinction which the following pages insist upon. A slacker is not a true idler because he* is engaged in the project of avoiding work, and as long as that remains the case, work's dominion remains unchallenged. Work rules even when, *especially* when, merely evaded.

The slacker bears more kinship to the procrastinator than to the idler. Procrastination, like boredom, involves a stall between first-order desires and second-order desires: both want to want to do something, but find they do not. They are stuck. The difference between them lies only in how they experience this stall, either as a burden of always

---

[*For undefended, and perhaps indefensible, reasons the male impersonal pronoun is used throughout this introduction.]

putting things off (procrastination) or as a burden of not being excited (boredom). The slacker in effect combines the two modalities into a single experience, under the rubric of evasion. But all three are prisoners of their failure: a failure that is in their own eyes as well as in those of their employers. We know that Russell has made this error of confusing slacking with idling because he uses the words *idling* and *laziness* interchangeably. That is the language of the work ethic, even if the attempted deployment is satirical. The idler is not lazy. Laziness is for slackers.

The true idler, by contrast, experiences no conflict or stall between desires and desires about those desires. He understands that not working and not-working are conditions that lie poles apart, and the genius of idling is not its avoidance of work but rather its construction of a value system entirely independent of work. Russell reforms the aesthetic Wildean idler into an ethical idler, judging work against itself, but only at the cost of undermining the overall project – an outcome Kierkegaard had himself anticipated with the sly juxtapositions of aesthetic and ethical that mark *Either/Or* with the stamp of genius.

The aesthetic version of the idler has long sanction, as the pages that follow will attest. And certainly the distinctive nineteenth-century urban-dandy idler, the *flâneur*, has much to recommend him. The *flâneur* makes his idleness into an art form, cultivating refinement of taste and exquisiteness of perception and judgment, if possible leavened by insouciant wit. From this standpoint, Russell's rehabilitation is out of order, an unfriendly amendment. It is only when work is thought characteristic of human life, and so work and idleness are opposed, that the latter may be considered bad or in need of defence. Kierkegaard makes amusement the most divine feature of humankind and so the poles are reversed: the enemy is not idleness but boredom. One does not become an unbored idler by slacking off work, or even by demonstrating the evils of work, even if it is uncontestably true that the work in question is not worth doing.

Then how? Well, certainly not by means of the cultivation of that sport known as 'leisure time' – another frequent misunderstanding. It is a truism, but one worth repeating, that the currently dominant conception of leisure time, with its increasingly frantic forms of rest and recreation, often involving shopping and forms of production-as-consumption, is self-defeating. Leisure time is worse than slacking. It suffers from the same dialectical assimilation because constructed in opposition to, and as the remainder from, work time.

But it is also, and worse, just a form of work in disguise. The slacker, while no true idler, at least knows that he is avoiding work. The leisure-time devotee is working but doesn't even know it! Leisure time is just work by other means. This is so both personally and systemically, or (to alter the terms) according to particular and general economies.

At the particular level, the leisure-time devotee is working because he is just as unfree in the face of leisure's imperatives as he was when confronted by those from work. The same desperation, eagerness to please, and comprehensive interminable insecurity are immediately observable. The slacker is surly and bored; the l-t devotee is crazed and frenetic. Both are empty at heart, but the l-t-d is delusionally convinced that he is happy, or at least pursuing happiness in one or more of its culturally sanctioned forms.

Hence the failure at a general level. Engaging in leisure time is ever an engagement with the cash nexus. This time is structured and disciplined by the nodes and conduits of a capital economy where cycles of production and consumption must work constantly in the direction misleadingly called 'growth'. In fact, what we call growth is really just the generation of a surplus. Such surpluses, as Georges Bataille notes, are generated by all economies, not just capital ones; the difference lies only in the manner by which a surplus is vented or off-loaded. Capital economies are like sharks: they must keep moving forward in order to live, understanding 'forward' here to mean in the direction of market expansion and product/service diversification. These vectors only exist if there are individuals available to make up the markets and purchase the products or services. The greatest and most important product of any capital market is the steady supply of consumers able to go shopping, try on shoes, view movies, listen to music, or any of a thousand other kinds of engagement with the economy. No leisure time, no consumption; no consumption, no economy; no economy, no life.

In this manner does consumption become ecstatic. The branded items are sought for their mystical qualities of establishing social and cultural position, not the lingering use values that might cling to them, in the form of protection from the cold or even aesthetic pleasure. These goods and services literally take us beyond ourselves, towards the selves we wish to be. So much is widely accepted. But, in a second mutation, ecstatic consumption is in turn amplified, via the media surround, into what Paul Virilio calls "hysterical commutation." Now the entire cycle of goods and services becomes biospherical force beyond which we cannot go, even in thought.

Consider a single timely example. Statistics recently reported in a liberal monthly magazine let us know, if we did not already, that the composition of gross domestic product is not even across nations. In the United States, 70 percent of the GDP is generated by consumer spending. It is a market economy in the most vivid sense, a vast bazaar of consumption. In emergent capitalist China, by contrast, only 35 percent of GDP is accounted for by consumer spending.

We need not linger here on the paranoid questions that this juxtaposition of numbers presumably aims to arouse: If they are not consuming, what are they doing? What about that vast consumer market we were promised? Why are we consuming so much relative to what we are producing? These questions are misplaced. Under conditions of hysterical commutation, not only is there no difference between production and consumption, there is no difference between a given GDP ('ours') and some other ('theirs'). The apparently reassuring clinical precision of GDP, that magic hard number, reveals the fundamental hysteria. GDP is not a measure of economic health, it is a measure of transactional heat. Every economic exchange contributes to it, no matter how rancorous or evil. A convicted corporate-executive serial killer, living on death row with the aid of elaborate life support, while undergoing a contentious divorce, is generating more GDP than most city neighbourhoods.

Economists get worried when the rate of GDP growth falls below some notional standard of 'health', usually around ten percent per year. This is exactly the wrong issue to consider. How is growth measured in the first place, and even more important, what is growth for? Those are the questions on which their attention should linger. Of course, that lingering would entail asking them to become philosophers instead of economists.

* * *

Lingering is what the idler excels at. These insights about productivity and growth, as well as work, show us why all previous philosophical defences of the idler before this one have not yet gone far enough – with two possible exceptions, one only partial, who will be discussed in a moment.

The idler is not a cultural rebel, some buy-nothing-day market refusenik. That refusal is caught in its own logic, a prisoner of protest. Nor is he an aesthete of his own sensibility, making experience of his singular life into a self-consumed work of art. Even the *flâneur* may be accused of excessive purpose, after all, directing his saunters around corners in pursuit of a glimpsed ankle or sound of merry-making. The aesthete and the cultural critic bear affinity to the idler, but the resemblance is and can only be partial. The idler is a much more comprehensive critic than is usually imagined, a dedicated overthrower of thought, not just culture or convention. He works at the limits of acceptability, perhaps at the limits of sense itself. The Germans have a word for it: idling must be considered in its true light as a *Grenzbegriff*, that is to say, a *threshold concept*.

So far, most of the claims made here have been by way of negation: we have been saying what the idler is not. What, then, is he? Is there a positive account of the true idler?

Well, sort of. The beginning of an apt description can be found in Bataille's classic, *The Accursed Share* (1949). Commenting on the fact that luxury becomes an acceptable but endless form of surplus-venting, Bataille notes the prison thus erected, the endgame version of the consumption as generally pursued. Luxury is just conspicuous waste, something that could be as easily accomplished by less malign and ego-entangled means. It crates ratchet effects, by which desire spirals ever upward, seeking more and more 'refined' (which is to say expensive) objects, but never coming to terms with the economy of desire as such. By contrast, "genuine luxury requires the complete contempt for riches," Bataille avers, "the somber indifference of the individual who refuses work and makes his life on the one hand an infinitely ruined splendor, and on the other, a silent insult to the laborious life of the rich."

Written just under a century after, this characterization might well put one in mind of Melville's Bartleby the Scrivener, from the 1853 story of the same name, with his quiet challenge to the work-based world of luxury: *I would prefer not to.* No mere preference despite the repeated formulation, Bartleby's stance is itself excessive, as the lawyer narrator of the story tells him; it is, however, an excess of principled withdrawal from the routinely generated excesses of the production-consumption cycle. Though the story is subtitled "A Story of Wall Street," according to Elizabeth Hardwick, "Bartleby is not a true creature of Manhattan, because he shuns the streets and is unmoved by the moral, religious, acute, obsessive, beautiful ideal of Consumption." And dies, as readers know, alone and starving, his face turned to the wall of a prison courtyard.

For the first time, perhaps, the depth of the idler's challenge begins to show: the challenge to his social-cultural surround, but also to himself as the agent of it. The idler must be at heart a loner, even if he sometimes or even often enjoys the company of others and pursues, with them, his idle course. There may exist dedicated collectives of unwork, creating conditions of idling's possibility; but the idler's philosophical path is a solitary one, an avenue of thought, which cannot be fully pursued except as a matter of inward contemplation.

There are numerous exits to failure on this avenue, some of them already mentioned. Consider in addition the surprising possibility that Kafka's Josef K., for example, is a sort of failed idler. K. wants to throw off the judgments of society, to find his own way, but instead he allows those judgments always to find him – such that, at the end of the mysterious process of coming before the law, it is he who helps his executioners turn the blade at the right angle to find his exposed breast. K. tries to idle and fails, undone by his own desires to understand and control his fate, to master a meaning which ever eludes him.

The same difficulty seems to afflict Aristotle, who is otherwise distinguished as one of the two philosophers who understand idling well. In Book X of the *Nicomachean Ethics*, Aristotle defends solitary contemplation as the most divine part of human life, the activity which brings us closest to the gods. This follows from Aristotle's more general commitment to leisure (*skholé* in the Greek, the etymological root of English 'school') as the basis of all culture. We do not live in order to work; we work in order to live. And the sphere of work remains, contrary to later ideas, in the realm of mere necessity: that which must be done so that we may engage our higher selves. This defence of leisure, in a work of ethics. is astonishing, at least to the ears of the later Western tradition.

Unfortunately, it is also in tension with Aristotle's larger insistence on virtuous action and the basically social nature of human life. Contemplation requires solitude, disciplined isolation from the imperatives of life in which we can ask, among other useless questions, what is the use of 'use'? What value, in other words, in the world's insistence on use-value? And yet, this isolation at the same time places the asker of such questions beyond the social pale, in the pre-social condition that Aristotle has elsewhere called the preserve of beasts and gods. This conflict between action and contemplation is not resolved by the *Ethics*, or at least not to any easy satisfaction. At best, it would seem that a cultivation of our god-like selves is a project for only part of the population or part of one's life. Aristotle seems caught: he wants to idle, because he knows that is where we will find our divinity; but he is afraid to make that, and not the textured happiness he calls *eudaimonia*, the life of virtue, his central conception of human flourishing.

* * *

Notice at this juncture a basic logical difficulty that has been, so to say, lingering behind us this whole time. To speak of *failure* in the cases of K. and Aristotle – to speak of 'true' idlers and lesser ones – is to suggest the companion possibility of *success*. This, however, introduces a strain of normativity into the project of idling that may seem contradictory. At its starkest, the problem issues in what may be called *The Idler's Conundrum*, which results when the project of idling, though shunning work, succumbs to its own kind of work ethic. Now the idler is once more a slave to an extraneous authority, something beyond his current whim. Take special note of this, for those among your circle with a penchant for *organized leisure*, as it is sometimes called, may be workers lurking behind a façade of idling.

There is likewise the related problem of *Positional Goods Creep*. Thorstein Veblen, in *The Theory of the Leisure Class* (1899), noticed how 'useless' goods and pursuits, especially when they involved the non-productive consumption of time, space. and goods, were especially characteristic modes of conspicuous consumption. "From the days of the

Greek philosophers to the present," Veblen notes, "a degree of leisure and of exemption from contact with such industrial processes as serve the immediate everyday purposes of human life has ever been recognized by thoughtful men as a prerequisite to a worthy or beautiful, or even a blameless, human life. In itself and in its consequences the life of leisure is beautiful and ennobling in all civilized men's eyes."

One might devote oneself to philosophical reflection in this time, as Aristotle hoped, but there is no requirement for it. Veblen takes note of how such time is actually occupied, namely in ostentatiously silly occupations that nevertheless retain a veneer of "ostensible use" or purpose: collecting rare editions or bibelots, cultivating some ancient sport, devoting generous attention to dress and manners. "[T]he gentleman of leisure] becomes a connoisseur in creditable viands of various degrees of merit, in manly beverages and trinkets, in seemly apparel and architecture, in weapons, games, dances, and narcotics. This cultivation of the aesthetic faculty requires time and application, and the demands made upon the gentleman in this direction therefore tend to change his life of leisure into a more or less arduous application to the business of learning how to live a life of ostensible leisure in a becoming way."

The idler would seem to be a paragon of this beautiful aristocratic life, since he wastes time with the best of them. If Veblen's Golden Age New Yorkers dismay our own desires, then reflect instead on Bertie Wooster, Gussie Fink-Nottle, Tuppy Glossop, Bingo Little, and Catsmeat Potter-Pirbright, those high-spirited *habitués* of P. G. Wodehouse's Drones Club, masters of cocktail shaker, jazz piano, and elaborate practical joke, often involving a betrothal. Arrogant or cheerful, such leisurely consumption of time and resources is the mark of social status in the emergent late-capitalist world, the idler leaps out as a king of social position, a man who conspicuously does not have to work, let alone work at anything difficult.

Observe the danger, however. Once viewed as a form of unequally distributed leisure, idling becomes just another luxury good such as a sailboat or pointlessly expensive shoes, allowing its possessor to establish competitive advantage over his rivals. Suppose he dismisses other luxury goods according to the insight entered earlier about general economies, he would seem trapped still in this inevitable economy of social position. Even if we detach leisure from money, and attach it instead to, say, learning, the position problem remains. John Kenneth Galbraith, writing in *The Affluent Society*

(1958), neatly set out the irony: "No one has really read very much if he hasn't read *The Theory of the Leisure Class* at least once." Inarguable. And yet, to be appreciated the book must be read carefully and slowly. "The book yields its meaning," Galbraith concludes, "and therewith its full enjoyment, only to those who too have leisure."

The solution to both the Idler's Conundrum and the problem of Positional Goods Creep lies in seeing that the language of effort and position are conspicuously out of place here. The true idler knows that using the adjective 'true' does not commit him to any special rules of idling, even his own. *Try not*, as Yoda said to impatient Luke Skywalker. *Do. Or do not. There is no try.* Or consider this exchange of idling wisdom from a still younger master:

> "Could you try not aiming so much?" he asked me, still standing there. "If you hit him when you aim, it'll just be luck." He was speaking, communicating, and yet not breaking the spell. I then broke it. Quite deliberately. "How can it be *luck* if I aim?" I said back to him, not loud (despite the italics) but with rather more irritation in my voice than I was actually feeling. He didn't say anything for a moment but simply stood

balanced on the curb, looking at me, I knew imperfectly, with love. "Because it will be," he said. "You'll be glad if you hit his marble – Ira's marble – won't you? Won't you be glad? And if you're glad when you hit somebody's marble, then you sort of secretly didn't expect too much to do it. So there'd have to be some luck in it, there'd have to be slightly quite a lot of accident in it."*

These paradoxical injunctions *not to try* and *not to aim* are precisely that which avoid luck. They dissolve in an instant the very idea of success – and failure. *There is no try!* This idle wisdom rescues the meta-logic of uselessness from its Aristotelian impasse, where action and contemplation are in tension.

The truest philosopher of idling, the second exception, is therefore not to be found in the tradition that follows Aristotle. This figure is perhaps not a philosopher at all, and likely not a singular personage but rather a tradition and body of work. The author of *Tao Te Ching*, sometimes called Lao Tzu, is the most comprehensive idler the record of discourse brings down to us. Some even more accomplished idlers surely existed without commit-

[*J.D. Salinger, "Seymour: An Introduction" (1959).]

ting their thoughts to paper even in poetic tangles; but Lao Tzu's legacy is there to inspire future generations where theirs is not. *Wu wei*, the doctrine of strength through weakness, the strength of the water that finds its way past any obstacle, is the idler's most profound truth.

"Blunt the sharpness," the *Tao Te Ching* advises. "Untangle the knots. Soften the glare. Let your wheels move only along old ruts." Idleness is not merely the condition of thought's possibility, as Aristotle thought. Lao Tzu knows that idleness is thought's transcendence of itself.

* * *

One last question must be broached by way of this introduction, yet it is one that can only be raised with considerable misgiving. What, if anything, is the justification for the present volume?

A glossary of terms defining and refining the concept of idleness would seem itself otiose, if not obtuse. All it can offer is the glib authority of that most tedious of reference works, the flat-footed alphabetical list. Surely there are more elegant efforts available in the idleness literature, essays and treatises of the sort already appropriated via citation? Moreover, are there not other recent introductory or expatiatory texts, compendia of quotations and apposite remarks, which defend the idle life to the present public? The answers are, respectively, *yes*; and *yes*.

Nevertheless, the offering before us will be misunderstood if it is taken as just another vocabulary gloss on just another topic – as if its list of terms might be consulted the way one looks, for example, at the back of a philosophy textbook to find out whether 'ontological' and 'deontological' are cognate terms. (Save yourself the trouble of wondering: they are not.) *Glossary* is defined as "a list of terms in a special subject, field, or area of usage, with accompanying definitions, often at the back of a book, explaining or defining difficult or unusual words and expressions used in the text." Any glossary is at best a subset of the dictionary, a boring list of words and their definitions set out according to that most banal of taxonomic schemes, the alphabet.

The present glossary is different. Not only the last word on idleness, it may also be the last word on glossing *tout court*. On the first point, simply note that there is no more idle text than this, with its refusal to offer complete sentences, its principled *flâneur*'s resistance to linear or extended thought, its marvelous Borgesian textual circularity, where terms seem forever bending back upon other terms, resisting mastery and completion. The frequent imperative use of *see*, traditional companion of insistent scholarly *consider*, *compare*, *contrast*, *note*, and *look*, here acquires the cumulative resonance of repetitive dementia. Every time the glossator directs you somewhere else, as if that would somehow help explain or complete a thought, the elbow-jogging nudges become all the more ridiculous. As if you need to *see* something else, let alone this other word or that one! You don't have to *see* anything! You can do just as you like!

In wonderful addition, consider on the second point that this glossary exists entirely without its accompanying text. It *is* the text; it does not appear at the back of anything. There is no back because there is no front!

This introductory text, whatever it is, does not count. Among other things, the present effort – if *effort* is even the correct word – enacts its own paradoxes and conundrums. Is it an essay, for example? The French gave us, via Montaigne, the word *essay*, whose root Latinate meaning is *attempt* or *try*. Is an essay that attempts a defence of not trying a failure or a success? Or is it perhaps not an essay at all?

Who knows? What we can say is that the urtext for which this glossary is definitive must be, in the end, life itself. And so this odd little alphabetical list, standing just on its own (or nearly so, given what you are reading right now), is revealed as both comprehensive and exemplary. Henceforth all further glossaries are superfluous because *everything you need to know about how to conduct a life* lies within these covers, if only sometimes by implication and omission.

Be warned, however: true idling is far from easy. Some claim that the capacity for it is unevenly distributed across human populations, perhaps according to distinctions impervious to philosophical intervention, such as youth. Meanwhile, versions of the Conundrum and the Creep complicate anyone's attempts to cultivate an idle life. You cannot try for it. And yet, the rewards are without compare, not for nothing called divine.

Evelyn Waugh neatly captures the complexity of the issue. Incandescent in his denunciation of sloth as the deadly sin most typical of late-modern life, he also delivered, in *Brideshead Revisited* (1945), one of the most moving paeans to languor in the language. Charles Ryder reflects thus on the idle summer he spent with angelic, doomed Sebastian Flyte: "The languor of Youth – how unique and quintessential it is! How quickly, how irrecoverably, lost!" Other traditional attributes of youth may be recaptured in later life, Charles muses, when we rouse ourselves to ambition or joy; "but languor – the relaxation of yet unwearied sinews, the mind sequestered and self-regarding, the sun standing still in the heavens and the earth throbbing to our own pulse – that belongs to Youth alone and dies with it." It is even possible that "the Beatific Vision itself has some remote kinship with this lowly experience; I, at any rate, believed myself very near heaven, during those languid days at Brideshead."

You may wish to thank the glossary's author for these gifts, but that is not recommended. He is a brilliant man, to be sure, and has shown himself a true friend to humanity; but he did no work on this book with the expectation of thanks or other recompense. He knows – after all, who better? – that a labor of love is not a labor. Anyway, how much work could it have been?

No, do not thank him. Thank yourself instead, for having the wisdom to procure this little volume, which shall certainly set you free if you have occasion properly to use it, which is to say not to use it at all.

The divine path is here sketched, dear friend. All that remains is for you to set foot upon it. Rest assured that, *pace* Ryder, it is not the exclusive province or privilege of youth. Realize, too, that it is not a path with a destination. It is not even a path. Indeed, realize that and *you are already there.*

THE IDLER'S GLOSSARY

For Tom Hodgkinson

THE IDLER'S GLOSSARY

JOSHUA GLENN

ABSENTMINDED: Losing yourself in thought, or in dreaming dreams – to the point of being unaware of your surroundings or actions – is a pleasure available only to the unemployed. (And the un-married, as Burgess Meredith discovers in an apoc-alyptic 1959 episode of *The Twilight Zone*.) But mindfulness, an engaged-yet-detached state of at-tentiveness that a select few idlers have managed to achieve, is even better than absentmindedness. See: DAYDREAM, FORGETFUL, THOUGHTLESS, MIND-WANDERING.

ACEDIA: To Aquinas, this melancholy condition [from the Greek for "absence of caring"], which afflicted solitary Christian monks and hermits, causing them to apathetically shirk labor and seek "undue rest," was a sin. Walter Benjamin later noted that acedia had reemerged, among sophisti-cated urbanites in 19th century Paris, as ennui; and Aldous Huxley would describe acedia as a "subtle and complicated vice," composed of boredom, sorrow, and despair at the futility of everything. See: APATHETIC, BOREDOM, ENNUI.

AESTHETICISM: Aestheticism gets a bad rap – it's too often mischaracterized (or practiced) as a retreat from the ugliness of everyday life into the otherworldly realm of art. However, as practiced by engaged aesthetes like Baudelaire or Flaubert, aestheticism is best characterized as a quixotic attempt to discover and create in everyday life the same opportunities for exaltation that an encounter with a work of art sometimes provides. See: EPICUREAN, FLÂNEUR, DETACHMENT, INDIFFERENCE, MINDFULNESS.

AESTIVATE: One hears tales of pre-WWII artists and writers aestivating – that is to say, spending the summer in rented seaside or mountain cottages. These days, however, only children, the ill, and the unemployed can get out of town for that long. See: VACATION.

AMBLE: The term was originally employed to describe the gait of a workhorse. So the difference between ambling, which sounds mellow, and purposeful movement isn't as great as it seems. The distinction is merely one of pace, not mode. See: PERAMBULATE.

AMUSEMENT: "Idle time-wasting diversion, or entertainment," claims an early definition. Idlers don't waste time, though, and time-wasters don't idle. It's important to distinguish between fun (exciting goings-on, gaiety, sport, drollery), which idlers are perhaps better disposed to enjoy than the rest of us, and mere amusement [from the Old French term meaning "to put into a stupid stare"], which typically involves staring – dazzled, like a deer caught in headlights – at some manufactured spectacle, whether a puppet show, TV program, or video game. See: FREE TIME, IDLENESS, KILL TIME, LEISURE ACTIVITY.

 ANABHOGYA-CARYA: In Hindu practice, *anabhogya-carya* is any purposeless activity that assists you in becoming detached from the fruits of your actions, and from the world of goal-oriented action generally. See: DETACHMENT, FIDDLE AROUND.

APATHETIC: The idler is too often accused – by socio-politically active acquaintances – of apathy. If the term means "without feeling or emotion," it would better be applied to those unfortunate souls who, precisely because they haven't dropped out of society, have been (to quote Philip K. Dick) "androidized." If, however, the term is used to mean "lacking interest or concern," we should note that the idler is deeply concerned with following his own subjective pathos, namely self-potentiation. See: ACEDIA, SLACKTIVISM.

ASCETICISM: Nietzsche is correct to call many instances of systematic self-discipline (celibacy, fasting) "life-denying." But the engaged ascetic – like Nietzsche himself – embraces life; for him, asceticism is a key tool in the project of self-overcoming. As the philosopher José Ortega y Gasset writes in *The Revolt of the Masses*, the epithet "noble" ought only to be bestowed upon those "for whom life is a perpetual striving, an incessant course of training. Training = *askesis*. These are the ascetics." See: EPICUREAN.

ASLEEP AT THE SWITCH: Why demonize those unfortunate souls who lose focus and zone out while on the job? No matter how focused their caffeinated colleagues may be, aren't they sleepwalking through life? See: ABSENTMINDED, DAYDREAM.

ASLEEP AT THE WHEEL: Driving is curiously like sleeping: During a road trip, time and space sometimes seem to become a dream-like projection of your own consciousness. Also, falling asleep at the wheel provides a helpful, if fatal wakeup call. See: INDOLENT.

ATARACTIC: Calm, serene, at peace with the world. Sounds nice, but note that the pseudo-medical term "ataraxia" [an Epicurean term meaning "freedom from confusion"] refers to that class of drugs which tranquilizes. Now, tranquility is an enviable state, but tranquilization is not! No matter what your shrink may have told you. See: LOTUS-EATER.

AUTONOMISM: Unlike Marxist organizers, who attempt to ameliorate or revolutionize the capitalist social order via the state, trade unions, and political parties, autonomists [from the Greek for "living by one's own rules"] in Italy, France, Germany, and elsewhere emphasize everyday, bottom-up resistance to capitalism, e.g., in the form of absenteeism, slow working, and socialization in the workplace. And, alas, violence. See: SKIVER.

AVOIDANCE: Avoidance can be a passive-aggressive means of abandoning your responsibilities. Still, the avoider – literally, "one who withdraws, vacates, i.e., so as to leave a place empty" – is not necessarily a coward. An obsolete, but important, definition of avoidance is: The act of clearing away received truths, in order to face the Void. See: BALK, DETACHMENT, GIDDY, QUITTER, UNWORK.

BACK-ROW HOPPER: Late 19th-century slang term for a barfly who frequents taverns looking for someone willing and able to buy him a drink. See: CADGER, SPONGER.

BACKSEAT DRIVER: British rhyming slang for "skiver," a lazy person. See: LAZY, SKIVER.

BAG Z'S: Distasteful contemporary slang for "take a nap." The phrase is distasteful because it represents the invasion of what Marxists calls exchange value into the sphere of sleep itself. Can Z's really be bagged? What price Z's? See: NAP, SLEEP, TIRED.

BALK: When a baseball pitcher fails to complete his prescribed motion, he is penalized for having "balked"; when a beast of burden balks, jibs, shies, and refuses to proceed, it is whipped. As Foucault explains, modern society disciplines those of us who experience moments of lucidity ("What the hell am I doing?") lest our madness come to seem sane. See: AVOIDANCE, BARTLEBY, DO-NOTHING, JIB, KICK BACK, OTIOSE, UNWORK.

BARTLEBY: Herman Melville's fictional office drone who will neither do his job nor quit it is both an inspiration to would-be idlers and a great puzzle. He isn't lazy, nor does he seem to resent or hate his employer (or want a different job), nor does he prefer a life of sensual pleasure, nor is he interested in making a spectacle of himself in order to help others see the light. He just "prefers not to" do anything. He has lost faith in the goodness of the world. This, it seems, is a form of passive resistance – against God. See: ACEDIA, BALK, KICK BACK, LACKADAISICAL, UNWORK.

BEAUTIFUL LOSER: The French poet Joë Bousquet, who wrote that "My life is externally the life of a reject, and I wouldn't want it any other way," was articulating the mantra of an evolved species (*homo superior*) whose members – like the geniuses in Olaf Stapledon's 1935 novel *Odd John*, or the teenage mutant heroes introduced in Stan Lee and Jack Kirby's *The X-Men* #1 (September 1963), or even the Argonauts who sought the Golden Fleece – are terrific at what they were born to do. But lousy at everything else. See: LOSER.

BEG: To ask bread or money in alms or as a charitable gift. Medieval Christianity was obsessed with the virtue of poverty; it was not uncommon to renounce all property

45

in order to live as Jesus and his disciples did. Perhaps the most likely derivation of "beg" is from Beghard or Beguine, a name given to the members of lay brotherhoods that arose in the Low Countries in the 13th century; they took no vow, and could come and go as they pleased. NB: A person who lives by asking strangers for aid is either lazy, mentally ill, or a saint. Don't assume that you can tell the difference. See: BUM, CADGER, SCAMP.

BENCHER: Slang term, from the 1930s, for someone who visits opium dens, but – oddly enough – only to observe, not smoke. Also used as a synonym for "benchwarmer." See: EPICUREAN, LOTUS-EATER.

BENCHWARMER: Colloquialism – dating to the late 19th century – for a substitute in a sports team, or any ineffectual person. Ever since the 1976 youth baseball movie *Bad News Bears*, which got us rooting for the uncoordinated benchers, this athletics-centric pejorative no longer carries quite so much shaming power, does it? See: AVOIDANCE.

 BIG ROCK CANDY MOUNTAINS: A hobo's idea of paradise, being an imaginary land "that's fair and bright,/Where the handouts grow on bushes and you sleep out every night," and –

most importantly – "where they hung the jerk that invented work." These lyrics are from a turn-of-the-century hobo ballad recorded in 1928 by Harry McClintock and popularized by Dorsey Burnette in the '60s. See: COCKAIGNE, HOBO, LUBBERLAND.

BLASÉ: Exhausted by enjoyment. Byron describes the blasé man as one whose "heart had got a tougher rind." It's a sad commentary on the triumph of middlebrow that an indifference to pleasure or excitement is nowadays considered sophisticated. Despite his unconcern for those things that matter to most people, the idler tends to run hot, to use bebop terminology, not cool. See: APATHETIC, CARELESS, ENNUI, NONCHALANT.

BLIND MONKEYS: Obsolete British expression referring to an imaginary collection at the Zoo: London jokesters supposedly told helpless and stupid types that they ought to apply for a job at the Zoo, leading the blind monkeys to evacuate their bowels. See: LOSER.

BON VIVANT: With whom would you rather sup, the persnickety gourmet or the gourmand – who simply loves good food and wine? The bon vivant is a diner-out, a raconteur, an appreciative guest. Open the door, let him in! See: SYBARITE, QUATORZIÈME.

BOONDOGGLE: Given the pointlessness of today's Boy Scouts, it's appropriate that this term, coined by an American scoutmaster to describe the braided leather lanyard made and worn by Scouts, has come to mean any time-killing or useless activity – particularly when performed by a sluggard on the public payroll. NB: The sociologist Robert K. Merton once claimed that intellectuals whose work lacks immediate practical application may suffer from the "boondoggling neurosis." See: DODGER, WHILE AWAY THE HOURS.

BOOTLESS: To no purpose. Must one wear boots in order to engage in non-useless, non-unprofitable, non-impractical activities? By no means! The term expresses a prejudice against non-laborers, and the use of it – in a post-industrialized society, anyway – smacks of fake authenticity. (You say that "boot," in this usage, is an Old English legal term meaning advantage, profit, or use? Never mind, then.) See: FLIP-FLOP, SLIPSHOD.

BOREDOM: Go ahead and blame your dull companions, but being bored [a slang term that appeared among London's smart set in the late 18th century, perhaps derived from the French for "triviality"] is your own fault. It's the state of being too restless to concentrate, while too apathetic to bust a move. The Situationist Guy Debord called boredom the "worst enemy of revolutionary activity." See: ACEDIA, AMUSEMENT, ENNUI.

BORN TIRED: Late 19th-century sarcastic description of a congenitally lazy person. Now that we've diagnosed Chronic Fatigue Syndrome, in which severe mental and physical exhaustion is "unrelieved by rest," according to medical authorities, and which may be worsened by even trivial exertion, this quip no longer sounds quite so funny. See: LAZY.

BUM: This pejorative, which came into general use during the Civil War, when it was applied to hangers-on and freelancers who followed General Sherman's troops, has long since been reappropriated, most notably in the American folk song, "Hallelujah, I'm a Bum." Unlike the pitiable fellow who sits in the same spot every day asking for a handout, the bum [from the German for "drifter"] roams about freely. See: BEG, HOBO, VAGABOND.

BUNKS MI RES: Rasta phrase meaning "take a nap." See: NAP.

CABBAGE: British slang for "sitting around doing nothing"; also slang for "catatonic." Not to be recommended to idlers, then. See: ATARACTIC, COUCH POTATO, TORPID.

CADGER: The art of imposing upon the generosity of others is a helpful skill to acquire, since going broke is the easiest way to obtain a great deal of free time. So long as a cadger [from the Scandinavian for "huckster"] is generous in turn (though not necessarily in kind), he ought not to be considered a deadbeat or sponger. See: MOOCHER, SKIMPOLE.

CAFÉ: Historically, one of the idler's favorite haunts – a public space in which intelligent conversation, witty repartee, and revolutionary plotting were uniquely possible. Try doing any of the preceding in a Starbucks, though; the laptop- and cellphone-users will abhor you. Online communities aren't as good, but they're better than nothing. See: HANG.

CALVINISM: In 1904, Max Weber argued that the religious aims of Calvinism, an ascetic Protestant sect, gave positive meaning to economic gain and investment; the rationalized spirit of capitalism grew out of the Calvinist work ethic. Over the years, he noted, meaning evaporated and rationalization trapped us in an "iron cage." Eighty years later, another Calvin, the 6-year-old co-star of Bill Watterson's "Calvin and Hobbes" strip, showed us a way out of the cage: truancy, scampery, and dreaming. See: TRUANT, SCAMP, DREAMER.

CAPRICIOUS: To be governed by caprice [which is either from the Latin for "hedgehog's head," or the Italian for "the frisk of a goat"] is to give in to your every fantastic whim, irresponsible vagary, or irrational desire. Of course, the idler knows better than to fill his every moment with turbulence and hurry. As long as you remain grounded to some extent, capriciousness will not burn you out. See: DESULTORY, ECCENTRIC, FLIGHTY.

CAREER: To be on a career path is to be stuck in a rut, like a wagon's wheel. As life has picked up pace, the term [from the Latin for "wagon-road"] has picked up connotations of speed and inexorability. By the late 16th century, it meant "racecourse" and, by extension, "full speed, impetus"; and by the 17th, it meant a "rapid and continuous course of action." In the early 18th century, "career" meant "a course of professional life or employment, which affords opportunity for advancement in the world." Advancement, that is to say, on an endlessly rotating merry-go-round. See: DESULTORY, HURRY, LABOR, WORK.

CAREFREE: In the 1938 musical of that title, Fred Astaire plays a psychiatrist who hypnotizes Ginger Rogers, a woman neurotically incapable of making up her mind. Astaire's plan backfires when Rogers begins to behave in a carefree fashion, resulting in one or two of the duo's most delightfully Hegelian dance routines. See: DETACHMENT, INSOUCIANT.

CARELESS: True, the idler is typically more spontaneous, chilled, and untroubled than the non-idler; so she might be described as careless, in the sense of "free of burdensome cares." But the idler is not necessarily careless in the usual sense of the term – negligent, derelict in her duties. For her sacred duty is *poiesis*, creation of herself and her world – and such work requires great care, indeed. See: DETACHMENT, DODGER, INSOUCIANT.

CASTLE BUILDER: Building imaginary castles, whether in Spain or in the air, is an addictive mode of fantasizing. Whether visionary schemers will accomplish great things or futz around for the rest of their lives cannot be predicted in advance. See: DAYDREAM.

CATNAP: The innkeeper who owns Old Deuteronomy, in T.S. Eliot's *Old Possum's Book of Practical Cats*, requires her customers to tiptoe out the back door whenever OD falls asleep, because "the digestive repose of that feline's gastronomy/Must never be broken, whatever befall." Our own naps should be guarded as zealously. See: DOG, NAP.

CHILL: Slang term meaning to "calm down." Popularized by the pioneering 1979 hip-hop song "Rapper's Delight," which helpfully instructed us that there's "a time to break and a time to chill/To act civilized or act real ill." So true! See: CHILLAX, RELAX.

CHILLAX: Is "chill" a synonym for "relax"? Apparently not, since the American vernacular now boasts a portmanteau word combining the two terms. This confirms the paranoid definition of "relax" which appeared in a preliminary version of this glossary nearly a decade ago: Chilling is something we all need to do, once in a while; relaxing, however, is strictly for laborers, and ought to be regarded as part of one's labors. See: CHILL, RELAX.

CLOCK: The machine-smashing Luddites were "bulls, hypnotized not by the flashing red cape but by the whir of machinery," argued the philosopher Sebastian de Grazia in his 1962 book, *Of Time, Work and Leisure*. "All the while the real enemy, the matador, was there behind, silent, imperturbable: the clock on the wall." See: DURATION, ENNUI, KILL TIME.

CLOCK-WATCHER: This term, which was coined twenty-five years after the invention of the factory time clock (which records the time on time cards pressed into it), ought not to be reappropriated by idlers. A clock-watcher is a slacker who really should, but won't, quit his job, drop out of school, and so forth. See: DODGER, KILL TIME, SLACKER.

COAST: As a form of locomotion, meaning "to glide, slide, skid, or skate along without propulsive power," coasting [from the Latin for "rib," which came to mean "a slope down which one slides"] is one of childhood's greatest pleasures. As a vernacular term meaning "to proceed easily without special application of effort or concern," though, coasting is a dangerous adult sport; sometimes an idler must pedal. See: AMBLE, DISTRACTED, LAZY.

COCKAIGNE: An imaginary country, the abode of

luxury and indolence. According to the OED, the derivation of the early 14th-century term – versions of which we find in Middle English, Old French, Spanish, and Italian – remains obscure, though it perhaps has something to do with "cake," since in Cockaigne the houses are made of pastry. See: BIG ROCK CANDY MOUNTAINS, LUBBER-LAND.

COMPLACENT: Despite her apparent disinclination to "better" herself, the idler can never be truly complacent [Latin for "pleased" (e.g., with oneself)], since she is forever seeking to invent and discover herself. Which tends to keep her on edge. See: APATHETIC.

COP OUT: Nineteen-forties slang term meaning "to escape" (e.g., from the cops, or other authorities), it has come to mean "give up an attempt" or "evade a responsibility." In the 1960s, a "cop-out" was a cowardly compromise or evasion, a retreat from reality. Paging Foucault! Idlers should reappropriate this anti-slacker term. See: AVOIDANCE.

COUCH POTATO: Idlers have rested supine on couches ever since upholstery was invented. But staring meditatively at the ceiling has been rendered much more difficult since the invention of the ever-tempting TV remote control. The channel-surfing lard-ass is a couch potato; let's call the sofa-based dreamer something different. See: SLUGGARD.

CUNCTATION: An obsolete term meaning "the action of delaying." One would like to see it resurrected, perhaps in order to describe Critical Mass, an event held on the last Friday of every month in cities and towns around the world, where bicyclists slow down or "cork" motor traffic on busy streets, in order to protest unfair cycling conditions. See: BALK.

DALLY: To converse, chat, flirt, or otherwise pass time in amusing repartee. (In Ireland: "blarney.") IMHO, IM'ing and text messaging are the ugly stepsisters of f2f dalliance. NB: The term has also come to mean "dawdle," or "loiter." See: SUPERFLUOUS MAN.

DANDYISM: Why do dandies take absurd pains with their appearance? Perhaps it's for the same reason that those who ended up surviving Stalin's gulags and Hitler's concentration camps are said to have carefully combed their hair and tied their shoes every day – because that's what it takes. Though some dandies are mere fops, then, for a select few, dandyism is an ascetic discipline: Baudelaire described it as "a system of gymnastics designed to fortify the will and discipline the soul." See: ASCETICISM, FLÂNEUR.

 DAWDLE: Paul Virilio, noting that Socrates was invariably late (*atopos*) to every appointment, suggests that philosophy itself is born of "idle (often pointless) curiosity, born of the disappearance of physical effort once this becomes unnecessary." And let's not forget Oscar Wilde's injunction that "punctuality is the thief of time." If you're always late because you've stopped to smell the roses, or chat with an acquaintance, you're a dawdler; if you're always late because you're multitasking, or because you like to remind your colleagues of how important you are, you're a jerk. See: FLÂNEUR, HANG, SLOW.

DAYDREAM: The imagination can be a powerful tool for liberation, claimed Simone Weil, but the daydreamer may be tempted into "filling up the void with compensatory illusions." Similarly, the painter Delacroix insisted that the imagination "remained impotent and sterile if it was not served by a resourceful skill which could follow it in its restless and tyrannical whims." Through dreaming while awake is inspiring, narcissistic daydreaming is enervating – and ought to be eschewed by idlers. See: ABSENTMINDED, CASTLE-BUILDER.

DEADBEAT: A 19th-century colloquialism for a slacker who sponges on his friends. More recently, it's come to mean "a father who lives apart from his children and doesn't support them financially." Either way, the term describes a cad. See: SKIMPOLE, SPONGER.

DEBAUCHED: Not merely given up to sensual pleasures, but fallen from a state of grace. To be debauched is to be seduced or corrupted from virtue, excellence, duty, chastity. This quasi-religious pejorative is derived from the French for "horizontal support beam." To her tsk-tsking detractors, the debauchee seems to lack an internal source of reinforcement; she has gone pear-shaped. See: DISSIPATED, SYBARITE, SLOUCH.

DESULTORY: From *desultory*, Latin for "a circus rider who leaps from horse to horse." This sounds exciting, but the word carries connotations of being trapped on a merry-go-round. Dr. Johnson wrote of a desultory friend that his art is "to fill the day with petty business, to have always something in hand which may raise curiosity, but not solicitude, and keep the mind in a state of action, but not of labor." Steadfastness is not always a virtue, and changeability need not always be erratic, but this seems an exhausting form of idleness. See: CAPRICIOUS, DISTRACTED, FLIGHTY.

DETACHMENT: Religiously speaking, detachment is not so much a form of aloofness or disengagement as it is a loving embrace of, and renewed fascination with the world – but from a position of critical, even ironic distance. As Krishna counsels in The Bhagavad-Gita, we should renounce the fruits of our actions without renouncing action itself. See: ACEDIA, APATHETIC, INDIFFERENT, NONCHALANT, WAITING FOR GODOT.

DEVIL-MAY-CARE: Wildly reckless, rollicking, free and easy. See: CARELESS.

DILATORY: The term comes from the past participle of the Latin word for "defer" or "submit" – i.e., as in a bureaucracy, where every question is referred to someone else, forever. Not, then, to be used as a synonym for dawdling. See: PROCRASTINATOR.

DILLY-DALLY: Dallying is a delightful, flirtatious way to pass the time. To dilly-dally, however, is to seesaw, zigzag, or shilly-shally – in other words, to act with trifling vacillation or indecision. As Dr. Livesey says, in *Treasure Island*, "There is no time to dilly-dally in our work." This is as true in our own lives as it is in a pirate yarn. See: DAWDLE.

DISSIPATED: The whole force of this term [from the Latin for "spend or use up wastefully or foolishly"] lies in the Protestant idea that you can somehow glorify God by accumulating stuff. But the idler prefers that part of the Bible in which Jesus asks us to consider the lilies, which toileth not, yet which are more beautiful than Solomon in all his splendor. Remember, too, the moral of Jesus' parable of the Prodigal Son: You aren't more beloved just because you've kept your nose to the grindstone. See: SYBARITE.

DISSOLUTE: Around the 14th century, actions marked by indulgence in things deemed vices began to be described as "dissolute," meaning that they tend to somehow dissolve, or disintegrate, the actor's very selfhood. This proto-totalitarian paranoia about "keeping it together" is, according to some postmodern theorists, the wellspring of such vices as racism, sexism, homophobia, and xenophobia. See: DISSIPATED, SYBARITE, UPTIGHTNIK.

DISTRACTED: The idler must struggle not only against the centrifugal force of distraction (which would shatter our hard-won state of mindfulness), but against the centripetal forces of what we might call "traction" (all those entities that would hold us back, keep us in our place). See: ABSENTMINDED, CAPRICIOUS, DESULTORY, INATTENTIVE.

DIZZY: It is everyone's duty to cultivate the voluptuous panic of vertigo, by staring into that void in which all the forms and norms of our daily lives are revealed as artificial constructs. As if that weren't difficult enough, you've got to revalue your values in light of this terrifying insight, and advance boldly into a new style of life. The problem with dizziness, as Sartre noted, is not how to keep from falling over the precipice, but how to keep from *throwing* yourself over it. See: AVOIDANCE, DISTRACTED, FLIGHTY, GIDDY.

DO-NOTHING: In politics, a do-nothing is an antiprogressive reactionary; elsewhere, though, he may be a saint. Oscar Wilde described his life's work as the "art of doing nothing," and insisted that for the brave idler living in a society that worships action, "to do nothing at all is the most difficult thing in the world." See: GOOD-FOR-NOTHING, IDLER.

DODGER: A dodger shirks his duties and evades his responsibilities neither for purposes of graft, nor out of fear, but simply out of an overwhelming distaste for labor. Think of Henry Miller ditching his career and family because he believed that "work . . . is an activity reserved for the dullard." Dodging can be an artful form of idling, and dodgers can be an inspiration. But the dodger who never quits the job or situation that he detests is not an idler but a slacker. See: BARTLEBY, KILL TIME, SKIVER, SLACKER.

DOG: Early 20th-century slang for "shirk labor." See: CATNAP.

DOODLE: Seventeenth-century British slang [derived from the German for "simpleton"] meaning "fool" or "lazy person." (As in the derisory song "Yankee Doodle.") This term ought to be reappropriated by idlers, since doodling – a 1930s colloquialism for half-assed drawing, done while your attention is elsewhere – can be an inspiring creative act. In Frank Capra's 1936 comedy, *Mr. Deeds Goes to Town*, Gary Cooper notes approvingly that "People draw the most idiotic pictures when they're thinking." See: DAYDREAM.

DOSSER: British slang term for someone who sleeps, or "dosses down," in any convenient place [from *dorsus*, Latin for "back"]. In the early 20th century, a tramp's female companion was known as a "dossie." In the 1940s and '50s, the term "dossy" was used to describe weak, ineffectual types – i.e., who'd rather doss than act. See: BUM, SLEEP.

DOZE: A term borrowed from Scandinavian languages, meaning to fall into a light sleep unintentionally from drowsiness, to be half-asleep. How depressing! Note that "dozy" is 20th-century military slang for "mentally sluggish, stupid, lazy." See: LAZY, TORPID.

DRAG: In its verb form, "drag" or "drag around" is 1960s slang for "waste time." The true idler's step never drags; freedom has put a spring in it. See: FLIGHTY, KILL TIME.

DREAMER: As Henry Miller puts it: "The dreamer

whose dreams are non-utilitarian has no place in this world . . . In this world the poet is anathema, the thinker a fool, the artist an escapist, the man of vision a criminal." Unlike the daydreamer, who escapes into romance and fancy because life has gotten the better of him, the dreamer believes that another world is possible – and that it only seems impossible to uptightniks. See: DAYDREAMER.

DRESS-AND-BREATH: Harlem Renaissance slang for a very lazy woman, i.e., whose only effort every day is to get dressed and breathe. See: LAZY.

DRIFTER: As *la dérive*, drifting was an essential component of the "revolution of everyday life" to those idlers par excellence, the Situationists. In order to free the senses from the "tyranny of the ordinary," Guy Debord and his comrades eschewed the usual motives for movement and allowed themselves to float across the urban terrain, driven hither and thither by the winds of desire. See: FLÂNEUR, FLIGHTY, SAUNTER.

DROP OUT: To disappear from public notice. Not at all the sort of thing that the publicity-hungry Timothy Leary had in mind when he urged 30,000 youth in San Francisco's Golden Gate Park to "Turn on, tune in, drop out." The former is challenging and adventurous; the latter merely hip and amusing. See: AMUSEMENT, QUITTER.

DROWSY: The etymological notion underlying the term seems to be "heaviness," as in eyelids made heavy by dreary, drizzly weather. The idler is instinctively opposed to the law of gravity; hence, she is unwilling to feel heavy, sluggish, or lethargic. See: DOZY, TORPID.

DUMMY: In auction or contract Bridge, the dummy is the player whose hand is being played by the declarer. Far from being useless to the other players, the dummy is now free to mix cocktails. Not to be confused with a dolt or blockhead. See: IDLER WHEEL.

DURATION: To the idler, nothing is so precious as what Bergson calls "duration": time divorced from productive operations, and dedicated instead to contemplation and reverie. See: DO-NOTHING, FREE TIME, INDOLENCE.

EASY-GOING: Comfort-loving, inactive, indolent; like a complacent horse. See: AMBLE.

ECCENTRIC: Although often dismissed as a "weirdo," because she has liberated herself from the stress-producing pressures of social conformity, the eccentric [literally, "out of the center," deviating from the norm] is, according to British psychologist David Weeks, generally both happier and healthier than we so-called normal types. See: CAPRICIOUS.

ENNUI: A lack of interest in your surroundings or activities. To be *ennuyé* is to be morbidly conscious of clock-time – one of the pillars of a culture based on toil, domination, and renunciation. Each tick of the clock says to the *ennuyé* individual, as it did to Baudelaire: "I am life, intolerable, implacable life!" Resignation to the subjective tyranny of time, insisted Herbert Marcuse, is "society's most natural ally in maintaining law and order, conformity, and the institutions that relegate freedom to a perpetual utopia." No wonder 19th-century rioters delighted in shooting at clocks. See: ACEDIA, BOREDOM, SPLEEN.

ENTROPY: In any natural or mechanical system, there exists an inherent tendency towards the dissipation of "useful" energy, and its transformation into "useless" energy. Something there is that does not love perpetual motion, or endless progress; the measure of that something's success in any given process or system is what we call entropy [from the

Greek for "turning," i.e., transformation]. See: IDLER WHEEL, USELESS.

EPICUREAN: The Greek philosopher Epicurus evolved a code of life and behavior which stressed the avoidance of pain, but his name has since been misused to describe those who actively seek pleasure (particularly, for some reason, through eating). Not every idler is a pleasure-seeker, and vice versa; in fact, many idlers are ascetics. Still, the history of idleness would be woefully incomplete were luxury- and sensuality-oriented idlers like Dr. Johnson, Oscar Wilde, and Lin Yutang left out, hence the inclusion in this glossary of those words used to describe pleasure-seekers. See: LUXURY, SYBARITE, VOLUPTÉ.

FAINÉANT: It's commonly assumed that this French term comes from *faire* (to do) + *néant* (nothing). But the OED claims that this is an etymologizing perversion of *faignant*, an Old French term for "sluggard" or "aristocrat." See: DO-NOTHING, SLUGGARD.

FART AROUND: In *The City of God*, Augustine laments that men who "have such command of their bowels, that they can break wind continuously at will, so as to produce the effect of singing," lost such impressive mastery over their bodies after Adam and Eve sinned. Despite this endorsement, and even though pathological distension of the bowel can result if you hold in flatulence, farting is *verboten* in offices. Whether you want to fart around literally or figuratively, then, you must first quit your job. See: FIDDLE AROUND.

FICKLE: Changeable, inconstant, unreliable – in a false, deceitful, treacherous way. Unlike the capricious person, who is enthusiastically ambivalent. See: CAPRICIOUS, DESULTORY.

FIDDLE AROUND: Not to be confused with killing time, to fiddle (or fart, futz, footle, potter, putter, or piddle) around is an act which in its very aimlessness is the embodiment of the philosophical ideal of leisure, and the Zen art of . . . well, anything. On the other hand, in the grasshopper-vs.-ant debate, the fiddling grasshopper isn't the hands-down winner. Nor do we praise Nero for fiddling while Rome burned. See: HALF-ASSED, TINKER.

FLÂNEUR: "Idle man-about-town": O, how much is contained in that definition! Contrary to what you may have heard about him, the flâneur does not suffer from ennui, nor is he blasé. Instead, he is an engaged aesthete who practices a kind of refined street theater, thumbing his nose at bustling urban crowds by loitering ostentatiously. For Baudelaire – who admired flâneurs like Nerval, who may or may not have walked a lobster on a pale blue leash – the "perfect flâneur" is that urbanite who is neither aloof from the crowd nor surrendered to it, but both at once; this "kaleidoscopic" faculty allows him to perceive the subtle eruptions of the infinite into the everyday. See: DRIFTER, IDLER, INDOLENT.

FLAZY: A recently invented slang term meaning fat and lazy. Some of literature's most entertaining slackers and idlers – from John Kennedy Toole's Ignatius J. Reilly to Gary Shteyngart's Misha Vainberg – have been on the heavy side. See: LAZY, JABBAENT.

FLIGHTY: To be flighty means to be skittish. But it also suggests capriciousness, which (as previously noted) is only a problem when you aren't properly "grounded" – since desultoriness, giddiness, and ennui may result. But after all, Nietzsche has written that "He who seeth the abyss, but with eagle's eyes – he who with eagle's talons graspeth the abyss: He hath courage." So: Leave

the ground behind and take wing! See: DESUL-
TORY, DIZZY, GIDDY.

FLIP-FLOP: Flip-flop, which used to mean "waf-
fle," was transformed into a pejorative synonym
[derived from flip flops, a favorite footwear of
idlers and slackers alike] for "procrastinate" – by
the sometimes less than completely understanding
spouse of the author of this glossary. Flip-floppers,
unite! See: BOOTLESS, PROCRASTINATE, SLIPSHOD.

FOOTLE: An endearing euphemism for the physical act of love, to footle is equivalent to, but more
romantic than, "fucking around." Such a delightful pastime ought not to be thought of as synonymous with wasting time. Quite the contrary.
See: FIDDLE AROUND.

FOOTLOOSE AND FANCY-FREE: An early 20th-cen-
tury term meaning "Having no attachments, especially romantic ones, and free to do as one pleases."
See: FREE TIME.

FORGETFUL: The daydreaming slacker is forgetful
[from the German for "losing your grip"], in the
sense of "a negligent failure to remember," to be
sure. The idler, on the other hand, from time to
time intentionally places over her own head what

Nietzsche calls "a firm dome of forgetfulness" – which allows her to forget both past and future, in order to be able better to concentrate on the present. See: ABSENTMINDED, DAYDREAM.

FORTY WINKS: Nineteenth- and early 20th-century slang for "a short nap, especially after dinner." This glossary can't possibly include every synonym for "nap," but this one is particularly interesting because the number 40 has a sacred or magical quality. See: NAP.

FOYL: Yiddish for "lazy." See: LAZY.

FREELOADER: A sponger, specifically one who loads up on the free food or drink available at a public occasion. Note that someone who rides public transportation without paying for it is called a "free-rider," which doesn't sound so bad. See: CADGER, SPONGER.

FREE TIME: Free time, in the sense of "freedom to," is electrifying and beautiful. But free time, in the sense of "freedom from," is merely restful and relaxing. Freedom-to time is what all idlers seek; it is a true state of leisure, in which actions are performed entirely for their own sake. Freedom-from time, on the other hand, is merely a vacation or a recess; i.e., it's a scheduled (and mandated) period during which we androidized humans can recharge our batteries. See: IDLENESS, LABOR, LEISURE, RECESS, RELAX.

FREEMAN: Originally, a man (or woman) who is personally free; i.e., a person who is not a slave or serf. Later, the term came to mean a citizen of a free society, as opposed to a tyrannical regime or totalitarian rule. Now that liberal capitalist democracies have become invisible prisons, though, a freeman is anyone who recognizes this fact. See: IDLER, INVISIBLE PRISON.

FUNKER: How good it would be to reappropriate this term [from an obsolete Flemish word for "paralyzing fear"], which contains within itself the holy monosyllable "funk"! But alas, no, this glossary needs a term that specifically refers to an individual who shrinks from his duties and responsibilities out of fear. And this one is it. See: DODGER.

FUTZ: Yiddish for "fart around." See: FART AROUND, FIDDLE AROUND.

GIDDY: In his existential psychoanalysis of Baudelaire, Sartre accuses that great idler of "bending over his own freedom and becoming giddy at the sight of the bottomless abyss." For those of us who practice avoidance (as a via negativa leading to the blissful state of idleness), giddiness is a very real and present danger: Instead of being creatively "dizzy," the giddy person is merely in a fruitless tizzy. See: AVOIDANCE, DIZZY, FLIGHTY.

GOLDBRICKER: Early 20th-century slang for a shirker, or lazy person. Ironically, the term was inspired by the example of Reed Waddell, a hard-working 19th-century swindler who hustled worthless bricks that he'd painted gold. See: DODGER, LAZY, SLACKER.

GOOD-FOR-NOTHING: Ah, Nothingness! In Buddhism, the "realization of the void" is the sudden, mind-blowing understanding that all things are intimately interconnected – and that, as a result, the universe is a million-fold more fecund and wonderful than you'd ever imagined. Call it enlightenment. The good-for-nothing slacker will always be with us; but perhaps some of us would-be idlers are good for Nothing? See: DO-NOTHING, LOSER.

GOOF (OFF): To spend time foolishly [from 20th-century slang for "stupid person"]. But is it always foolish to dawdle, or play truant? Sometimes "goofers" – as citizens who ignored orders to seek shelter during air raids were called in the 1940s – catch a glimpse of the way things really are. Philip K. Dick's paranoid postwar stories in which shelter-dwellers are bamboozled by their own government cast the goofer in a heroic light. See: DODGER.

GOVERNMENT STROKE: Nineteenth-century Australian slang for the deliberately minimal rate at which a convict laborer performs his mandated duties. It has since come to mean "lazy effort," generally. The parallels between prison life and white-collar office culture would be funny if they weren't so tragic and depressing. See: DODGER, SLACKER, INVISIBLE PRISON.

HALF-ASSED: When Confucius's grandson, Tsesse, claimed that the human spirit is happiest when we leave things half-done, was he talking about half-assery? Probably not. The slacker who coasts through school, or skims reports and delegates responsibility so well that he gets promoted at his job, is half-assed. Half-assery is, in fact, a world-historical secret of success; a prophecy found in Arthur Golding's 1587 translation of *Woorke concerning the trewnesse of the Christian religion* warns that

"A Halfeasse of Persia shall come and make us his thralles." Sounds all too likely. See: FIDDLE AROUND.

HANG (OUT): Nineteenth-century British, and 20th-century surfer, colloquialism for "while away the hours with friends." Benjamin Franklin put an activist twist on the phrase (avant la lettre) when he punningly urged his fellow Declaration of Independence signers, "We must, indeed, all hang together, or most assuredly we shall all hang separately." See: CHILLAX, DAWDLE.

HEBETUDINOUS: This excellent, medical-sounding synonym for "lethargy," as in "dullness," ought to be applied to slackers, not idlers. See: LETHARGIC, TIRED.

HEDONIST: The Greek word for "pleasure" is derived from the word for "sweetness," which is why we ought only to describe as "hedonistic" that way of life which takes the pursuit of sweet pleasures as its highest goal. Those who prefer bitter pleasures – Lin Yutang, for example, writes that the most significant inventions in the history of mankind are "smoking, drinking, and tea" – must look elsewhere for an adjective. See: EPICUREAN.

HIT THE SACK: Also known as "sacking out," this is a World War II-era slang expression for going to sleep. It carries unpleasant, even militaristic and violent connotations of sleeping-because-you-have-been-soldiering-on-to-the-point-of-exhaustion. See: SLEEPY.

HOBO: A 19th-century term that originated in the American West, among train-hopping laborers who preferred it to "tramp." To the well-off, "hoboing it" meant spending the summer on the road, fancy-free. But during the Depression, some two million men and women hoboed out of dire need, forming a nation within a nation with its own currency, signs and symbols, songs, and folklore. Preston Sturges' great 1941 film "Sullivan's Travels" explores the dark side of hobo culture; more recently, John Hodgman's satirical almanac, *The Areas of My Expertise*, popularized its lighter side. See: BUM, TRAMP.

HOLIDAY: Until the 16th century, there wasn't a marked distinction between a consecrated day or religious festival, on the one hand, and a day of recreation and mere amusement, on the other. Then, for a couple of hundred years, the two were quite distinct. Now, under advanced capitalism, holidays and holy days have once again become indistinguishable: They're both too-short periods of cessation from labor. See: VACATION.

HOMER: Slang term for work done strictly for personal benefit (i.e., for home) while ostensibly engaging in wage labor. The French term for this sort of thing is *la perruque*. Slackers with a little spirit make homers; slackers with a lot of spirit quit, and become idlers. See: DODGER, SLACKER.

HURRY: A 16th-century term originally meaning "agitation, bustle, disorder, tumult." Though the idler is always prepared to act quickly – indeed, she is quicker off the mark than the rest of us – undue or immoderate haste only leads to perturbation and chaos. See: CAREER, CUNCTATION, DAWDLE.

IDLE HANDS: They're the Devil's tools, or playthings, or workshop, according to colloquial metaphor. It's true: Individuals who are bored, killing time, or shirking are more likely to get up to mischief or into trouble than either laborers or idlers. See: BOREDOM.

IDLENESS: "Idleness so called, which does not consist in doing nothing, but in doing a great deal not recognized in the dogmatic formularies of the ruling class, has as good a right to state its position as industry itself," insisted a young Robert Louis Stevenson. How right he was! Idleness [from the Old English word for "worthless, useless"] may look to the untrained eye like laziness, slacking, killing time. Unlike slacking, though, idling is not the opposite of working hard, but is instead a rare, hard-won mode in which your art is your work, and your work is your art. See: FREE TIME, LEISURE, USELESSNESS.

IDLER: "There are plenty of lazy people and plenty of slow-coaches, but a genuine idler is a rarity," writes Jerome K. Jerome, in *Three Men in a Boat* (1889). "He is not a man who slouches about with his hands in his pockets. On the contrary, his most startling characteristic is that he is always intensely busy." In his 1998 poem "Not the Idle," Carl Dennis praises the same rare type: "It's not the idle who move us but the few/Often confused with the idle, those who define/Their project in terms so ample/That nothing they ever do is a digression . . . ." Despite our tendency to use "idle" as a pejorative meaning "lazy" or "useless," the idler is neither. See: FREE TIME, FREEMAN, IDLENESS, OTIOSE.

IDLES, THE: Seventeenth-century slang for laziness,

especially in the guise of illness. When a laborer feigned sickness, his coworkers would say he'd "come down with a case of the idles." Also: To "work at Idle Hall" meant to be unemployed. The author of this glossary, of course, believes that idleness is anything but lazy. See: DODGER, SLACKER.

IDLER WHEEL: By moving in a direction contrary to the motion of the rest of the machine of which it is a part, the idler wheel performs the vital function of transferring energy from one cog to another. There's a lesson in here, somewhere, about the subtle usefulness of the idler to society, don't you think? But it's a distastefully utilitarian line of thought, so perhaps we ought not to pursue it. See: DUMMY, ENTROPY.

INACTIVE: Sartre writes that "all human activities are equivalent, on principle doomed to failure. Thus it amounts to the same thing whether one gets drunk alone or is a leader of nations." But just try telling that to your boss, or spouse. Or to the authorities! Guy Debord noted that of all the offenses committed by the Situationists, the one considered most threatening by the police was their "prodigious inactivity." See: BALK, KICK BACK.

INATTENTIVE: Slackers don't pay close attention while on the job, and we can certainly sympathize. As Simone Weil discovered, though, attention is not a matter of holding our breath and wrinkling our brow, but "suspending our thought, leaving it detached, empty, and ready to be penetrated by the object." This kind of attention, or mindfulness, is only possible in the state of perfect idleness. See: ABSENTMINDED, DISTRACTED, FORGETFUL.

INDEPENDENT: "I am extremely idle and extremely independent both by nature and by intention," writes Michel de Montaigne. "This has made me slack and unfit for the service of others," he continues. "It has made me useless to any but myself." How proudly he claims these Renaissance-era pejoratives! We should all do the same. See: FREE-MAN.

INDIFFERENT: Not to be confused with apathy, indifference is a rare and wonderful mode of existence in which you are simultaneously engaged with and detached from the phenomenal word, as in Camus's longed-for "passionate world of indifference." The philosopher is indifferent; the teenager apathetic. See: CARELESS, DETACHMENT.

INDOLENT: For Keats, neither Love nor Ambition

nor even Poesy contain joy "so sweet as drowsy noons,/And evenings steep'd in honied indolence." Indolence [from the Latin for "feeling no pain"] may resemble laziness or sluggishness, but it's less a physical aversion to activity or effort than it is a romantic repudiation of what Keats calls "the voice of busy common-sense." See: DURATION, FREE TIME, IDLENESS, KEF, OTIOSE.

INERT: The idler sometimes appears to be inert [from the Latin for "unskilled, and therefore unable to work"]. In the first installment of "The Idler," a twice-weekly essay launched in 1758, Samuel Johnson reassured his readers that "the diligence of an Idler is rapid and impetuous, as ponderous bodies forced into velocity move with violence proportionate to their weight." See: FLAZY, SLOTHFUL.

INSOUCIANT: The mien of the person practicing engaged detachment, or passionate indifference, is neither earnest nor smirking – for these indicate a feeling of self-superiority that true detachment precludes. The light-hearted unconcern of the insouciant [a French word derived from the Latin for "not agitated"] philosopher or idler ought not to be confused with cynicism or superciliousness. See: CARELESS, DETACHMENT, NONCHALANT.

INTELLECTUAL: A man whose wife has a job. (That's my father's joking definition, anyway.) The freelance or public intellectual gets no respect from his family and friends, but ever since the publication of Russell Jacoby's *The Last Intellectuals* in 1987, we're at least aware that public discourse and the life of the mind are poorer without them. See: BOONDOGGLE, FREEMAN, LUFTMENSCH.

INVISIBLE PRISON: The German poet Heine once called America – where political, economic, and religious tyranny had been replaced by an indirect domination that 150 years hence would be named "neoliberalism" – a "monstrous prison of freedom" whose inmates were shackled by "invisible chains." European intellectuals, including members of the so-called Frankfurt School, French postmodernists, and Slavoj Zizek, have echoed this sentiment. Until the collapse of Soviet Communism, few Americans took them seriously; now, more and more do. See: DANDYISM, FREEMAN, GENERAL STRIKE, SLOTHFUL.

JABBAENT: An invented slang term meaning "as sluggish and gross as Jabba the Hutt of the *Star Wars* movies series." See: FLAZY.

JIB: To jib is to refuse to go forward, as when a jib

sail flaps from side to side. It's helpful to think, here, of Kierkegaard's description of the disorienting flapping motion that the ironist's contracting and expanding self seems (to him) to make. Not every idler is an ironist, and vice versa; but there is a tremendous amount of overlap. See: BALK.

KAROSHI: The Japanese term for "death from overwork" – for decades, the Japanese government has been trying, and largely failing, to set limits on work and on overtime – will surely become as common in Western countries as "karaoke." See: ASLEEP AT THE WHEEL, LABOR.

KEF: In the Middle East, kef is a state not of lassitude, but indolence – the enjoyment of idleness. Supposedly backward Middle Eastern cultures don't frown upon a fellow who "does kef" in public. How utterly enlightened! See: DURATION, FREE TIME, INDOLENT.

 KICK BACK: Although to kick back means to take it easy, it would be better employed as shorthand for fighting for your right to be idle: kicking against the pricks that stand between you and freedom, kicking over the traces, and kicking out the jams. See: BALK.

KILL TIME: "Filling," "passing," "wasting" time: Before 1887, no one ever considered disrespecting time in this fashion. That's the year that the time clock was invented, after which "duration" – Bergson's term for time which is full and rich, and not divided artificially – began to be guarded jealously by those in power. Ever since, wage slaves have confused clock time with time itself, and have longed to kill it. See: FREE TIME, LABOR, DURATION.

LABOR: In the course of uncovering the structures of human action *qua* existence and experience, the philosopher Hannah Arendt argued against Marx, who'd elevated labor to a position of primacy in his vision of the highest ends of human existence. Whether you are a baker or a lawyer, insisted Arendt, labor is subject to nature and necessity; it is therefore never-ending, and a form of slavery no matter how well paid. See: WORK, WAGE SLAVERY.

LABORER: "I can't go to work/The boss is a jerk," according to a song found on the first EP by the Los Angeles hardcore punk act Black Flag. All labor (as opposed to work) is Sisyphean, and all laborers are – or long to be – slackers. True, this is not the highest goal to which men can aspire . . .

but who can blame them for doing so? See: SLACKER, WORK.

LACKADAISICAL: Although often used as a synonym for "carefree" or "insouciant," this term is derived from "lackaday," as in "alas, the day." Proust-like, the lackadaisical slacker – crippled by nostalgia for times past – lacks the will to get out of bed. See: BARTLEBY, BLASÉ, ENNUI, OBLOMOV, SPLEEN.

LAGGARD: Because life was once nasty, brutish, and short, and everyone had to keep pace with his nomadic tribe or risk being eaten by wild animals, every language has its own way of contemptuously describing the individual who falls behind. "Laggard" is how the Norwegians say it. NB: Those of us who live in advanced capitalist societies sometimes find that the more we lag, the less likely we are to die young, of overwork. See: DAWDLE, KAROSHI.

LANGUID: Languor is an enervated weakness or weariness of the body or mind. The languid [from the Latin for "weak"] neurasthenic – who cannot bear to experience any of the human passions, and who languishes so attractively, has given a bad name to the indolent idler, who may be perfectly fit and full of energy. (Note that Oscar

Wilde's infamous languidness was just a pose.)
See: LISTLESS, SLUGGISH, SPLEEN, TIRED, TORPID.

LASSITUDE: The word comes from the Latin word for "tired." Note that the same Latin word also gives us "late" – as in "too tired to get there on time." See: DAWDLE, TIRED.

LAXITY: Looseness, slackness. To describe someone or something as wanting firmness, strictness, or precision might reflect poorly on the describer, not the describee. But if someone or something wants tension, then for God's sake, tighten it up. See: SLACKNESS.

LAYABOUT: We might take this pejorative as a synonym for "slacker," except for the fact that it was appropriated by Paul Morand, author of the never-completed manual *For the Use of the New Idle*, who liked to boast that he belonged to "the great secret society of layabouts enjoying the scorn of a world which works too hard." See: LOSER.

 LAZY: This term [from the German for "slack"] has largely replaced the native English terms "slack" and "idle" as the preferred way to express the concept "averse to labor." But we must distinguish, with Aristotle, between a deficiency in will and spirit (*aergia*), on the one hand, and abstention from worldly activities in order that one may be more meditative (*skhole*), on the other. The former leads to laziness, the latter to idleness. Paul Lafargue's 1883 tract *The Right to Be Lazy* urges the working class to demand a three-hour day in the name of *skhole*, not *aergia*. See: LANGUID, SLUGGISH, TIRED, TORPOR.

LEISURE: Those of us who live in advanced capitalist societies worship our "leisure time." However, as Aristotle notes, because this so-called leisure [from the Latin for "being permitted"] is made necessary by work, although it can produce a feeling of relief, it's a form of labor. Only time passed doing that which is desirable for its own sake (e.g., the hearing and making of music and poetry, conversation with friends, contemplation), Aristotle insisted, can be described as "leisure." See: FREE TIME, IDLENESS, OTIOSE.

LEISURE ACTIVITY: "It would be tedious to mention individually those who have spent all their lives playing draughts or ball, or carefully cooking themselves in the sun," wrote Seneca, in *On the Shortness of Life*. "They are not at leisure whose pleasures involve a serious commitment."

See: AMUSEUMENT, FREE TIME, LEISURE, VACATION.

LETHARGIC: Whereas the *ennuyé* person is afflicted with an oppressive sense of the too-muchness of existence, the lethargic person [the River Lethe, in Greek mythology, is the river of oblivion] is rendered stagnant by the dullness of it all: He is dead-while-alive. See: BOREDOM, ENNUI, TORPID.

LIBERTINE: A libertine [from the Latin for "free"] is a freethinker, especially in religious (these days, read: cultural) matters, and struggles to free herself from the invisible restraints of all prevailing conventions. Because free thought is anathema to the guardians of the dominant discourse, "libertine" has come to be a synonym for "leading a dissolute life"; it would be a mistake to assume that all libertines do so. See: FREEMAN, KICK BACK.

LICKDISH: Archaic term for a freeloader able to sniff out a major meal and show up uninvited; also known as a "smellfeast." See: CADGER, FREELOADER, SPONGER.

LIE-ABED: "Everybody seems to think I'm lazy," sings John Lennon in the lie-abed anthem "I'm Only Sleeping." He continues: "I don't mind, I think they're crazy." After becoming semi-paralyzed, the French poet Joë Bousquet decided that spending his life confined to bed (à la Proust) might be a great blessing. Doing so helped him realize, he said, that "the world is larger in me than in the world." See: LOLL, RECUMBENT, SUPINE.

LIGGER: HE: "Who do you know at this party?" SHE: "No-one. I'm just ligging." A ligger is a freeloader, a gate-crasher, a hanger-on. The English magazine *New Music Express* popularized the term in the 1990s. See: FREELOADER.

LIMPSY: "My illness unblocked me, it gave me the courage to be myself," writes Nietzsche. "Am I a philosopher? Who cares?" So speaks a sick man who isn't the slightest bit limpsy – a vernacular 19th-century term describing a poor soul who looks "as if there wa'n't no starch left in her," as Harriet Beecher Stowe once put it. See: INDOLENT.

LISTLESS: Destitute of relish for some specified object or pursuit; unwilling to move, act, or make any exertion; lacking "list" (lust, appetite, craving, desire) for life. See: LANGUID.

LOAF: The term, which originally meant "traveling around aimlessly," is likely derived from a

German term "applied by the steady and phlegmatic people to men who are irregular and unsettled in life," according to a 19th-century study of Americanisms. See: BUM, VAGABOND.

LOITER: To linger indolently on the way when sent on an errand; to waste time when engaged in some particular task; to dawdle with intent to commit a felony. The term's etymology – it's from the Dutch for "wag about (like a loose tooth)" – suggests that loitering is flânerie in mufti; or perhaps flânerie is loitering in drag. See: FLÂNEUR.

LOLL: To lean idly; to recline or rest in a relaxed attitude, supporting oneself against something. Lin Yutang suggests that we can achieve "the highest wisdom of living" by alternating between the "absolutely erect working posture" and "the posture of stretching ourselves on a sofa." See: PUT YOUR FEET UP, RECUMBENT, SLOUCH, SUPINE.

LOLLOP: To go with a lounging gait, bob up and down, proceed by clumsy bounds. The term appears to be an onomatopoeic extension of "loll," when that term is used to mean "hang down loosely, droop, dangle." See: AMBLE, EASY-GOING, SAUNTER.

LOSER: Whether he succeeds or fails, the true loser is the man or woman who enters a race that isn't worth the effort. Quitters are winners. See: BEAUTIFUL LOSER, QUITTER.

LOTUS-EATER: According to Homer, among other mythopoets, there was once a race of people from an island near North Africa who spent every day lost in the dreamy indolence produced by eating the narcotic lotus blossom. Aldous Huxley's dystopian novel *Brave New World* predicted that, one day, western governments would legalize a hedonistic drug (Soma) in order to control the population through pleasure. See: INDOLENT.

LOUNGE: To move, recline, or pass time indolently. To lounge [the term is of obscure origin] is to engage in the most spectacular form of indolence as yet known to us. Unlike the flâneur, who loiters in the public square, the lounger – not to be confused with "lounge lizard," who merely poses as a lounger – prefers to outrun ennui in the cool, dim depths of a red-velvet-swathed . . . lounge. During the cocktail music revival of the 1990s, this much-neglected term made an astonishing comeback. See: FLÂNEUR, INDOLENT, INSOUCIANT.

LUBBER: A lazy, thriftless individual. "Abbey lubber" is an obsolete term of contempt for an able-bodied fellow who grows fat on the charity of religious houses. See: CADGER.

LUBBERLAND: From a 1685 broadside ballad titled "An Invitation to Lubberland," we learn of an imaginary country where "There is all sorts of Fowl and Fish,/With Wine and store of Brandy;/Ye hae there what your hearts can wish:/The Hills are Sugar-Candy." Highly appealing to the chronically lazy. See: BIG ROCK CANDY MOUNTAIN, COCKAIGNE.

LUFTMENSCH: A Yiddish term [*luft* (air) + *mensch* (person)] that can refer either to an impractical visionary who wanders from place to place, starving his body in order to free his mind, or to a person without a definite occupation. In the 1960s, older New York Intellectuals sometimes called revolutionary students *Luftmenschen*. In a more positive vein, freelance or public intellectuals – i.e., thinkers who scrape by outside the groves of academe – have also been called *Luftmenschen*. See: BOONDOGGLE, INTELLECTUAL.

LUXURY: Originally a term denoting sinful self-indulgence, luxury [from the Latin for "abundance"] has only in the past couple of hundred years come to acquire positive connotations of costliness and comfort. Some wise idlers – Lin Yutang, for example – continue to counsel that moderation and balance in all things is the best route to true happiness. More radical idlers, like Georges Bataille, argue that "genuine luxury requires the complete contempt for riches." See: DURATION, EPICUREAN, SYBARITE, VOLUPTUARY.

MALINGERER: Military term meaning "one who pretends or exaggerates illness in order to escape duty or work." Possibly derived from a misspelled version of a 16th-century French word meaning "sickly, ailing." See: DODGER, IDLES, SLACKER.

MEANDER: The Maeander River, which flows through Turkey into the Aegean, was famous in ancient times for its winding course – which is how its name became a synonym for wandering aimlessly or casually, without urgent destination. See: SAUNTER.

MEGEGE: Yiddish for "dawdler," which isn't necessarily a bad thing. A "shmegege," on the other hand, is a dawdler who is also an idiot. See: DAWDLE.

MICAWBERISH: Is anyone's heart so hard that it doesn't go out to Micawber, the secret hero of *David Copperfield*. Micawber – portrayed brilliantly by W.C. Fields in the 1935 movie adaptation of the Dickens novel – lives in optimistic expectation of better fortune, but won't lift a finger to make it come any sooner. See: LOSER, POCOCURANTE, SLACKER.

MIND-WANDERING: Aquinas believed that mind-wandering was a "daughter sin" of acedia. But just as the melancholy concomitant with acedia can give us insight, so too can mind-wandering expand our horizons. It's a lot less project-oriented than "brainstorming," too. See: ABSENTMINDED, DREAMER.

MINDFULNESS: "The important thing in our understanding is to have a smooth, free-thinking way of observation," notes Zen master Shunryu Suzuki. "Thinking which is divided in many ways is not true thinking. Concentration should be present in our thinking. This is mindfulness." See: ABSENTMINDED, DISTRACTED, INATTENTIVE, SIT BACK.

MINIMAL EFFORT: The slogan of the International Institute for Not Doing Much, a fictional organization dedicated to the eradication of multitasking. See: CUNCTATION.

MOOCH: British colloquialism for "kill time," "loiter aimlessly," "walk in an extremely casual fashion," or "play truant from school in order to pick blackberries." Derived from an obsolete term, "mitch," meaning "skulk," "absent oneself without authority," or "play truant from school." In the 19th century, "mooch" became a slang term for "sponge" or "scrounge." See: AMBLE, CADGER, LOITER, MOOCHER.

MOOCHER: Nineteenth-century slang for a slacker "who tries to get something free of charge," though without a salesman's poise, and therefore without success. Cab Calloway's 1931 jazz song "Minnie the Moocher" describes a woman who dreams of living with the King of Sweden, because he'll provide her with all the marijuana that she can smoke. According to Henry Miller, when performed without squeamishness or reservations, mooching is both exhilarating and instructive for idlers. See: CADGER, SKIMPOLE, SPONGE.

MOSEY: Nineteenth-century Western US slang for "walk in a leisurely or aimless manner." Possibly derived from the obsolete British regional colloquialism "mossy," meaning "confused, bewildered, fuddled through drinking alcohol." See: AMBLE.

MURRUMBIDGEE WHALER: Australian loafer who works for about six months of the year – i.e., during shearing and harvest – and camps the rest of the time in the region of the Murrumbidgee River, fishing and begging. See: BUM, HOBO, LOAFER, TRAMP.

NAP: "A beautiful nap this afternoon that put velvet between my vertebrae," writes Henry Miller. "Gestated enough ideas to last me three days." Not to be confused with being asleep at the switch or the wheel, or with dozing half-awake at your desk, to sleep lightly and briefly during the day, when everyone else is busy at the office, is the kind of pleasure even the most ascetic of idlers can endorse whole-heartedly. See: DOZE, TIRED.

NEGLIGENT: Inattentive to duty, heedless, neglectful. The slacker is negligent; not the idler. See: CARELESS, FORGETFUL, INATTENTIVE.

NEVER, DO A: Nautical slang for shirking. See: DODGER, SLACKER.

NEVERSWEAT: Nineteenth-century colloquialism for "lazy person," or "one whose job requires little effort." Speaking of sweat, the social critic Mark Greif helpfully points out that "Nothing can make you believe we harbor nostalgia for factory work but a modern gym. The lever of the die press no longer commands us at work. But with the gym we import vestiges of the leftover equipment of industry into our leisure. We leave the office, and put the conveyor belt under out feet, and run as if chased by devils." See: DODGER.

NONCHALANT: Etymologically, the term comes from the French expression for "not hot under the collar." This is not the same thing, however, as being "cool," if by that term you mean blasé, sophisticated indifference. Nonchalance is instead a stylish form of engaged detachment, or sprezzatura. See: DETACHMENT, INDIFFERENT, INSOUCIANT.

NONMEETING: A term introduced by Fernando Pessoa, in his 1929 poem "Ah, the Freshness in the Face of Leaving a Task Undone." Pessoa writes: "It's too late to be at either of the two meetings where I should have been at the same time . . ./No matter, I'll stay here dreaming verses and smiling in italics./This spectator aspect of life is so amusing!/I can't even light the next cigarette . . . If it's an action,/It can wait for me, along with the others, in the nonmeeting called life." See: DODGER, FIDDLE AROUND, KEF.

OBLIVIOUS: Unaware of, or unconscious of something. From the Latin for "forgetful." The slacker is oblivious; the idler mindful. See DAYDREAM, INATTENTIVE.

OBLOMOV: Oblomov, the lethargic protagonist of Goncharov's 1859 novel of that title, is such a well-realized and sympathetic character that his name has become synonymous with "beautiful loser." However, Oblomov's indolence is not principled; he's not an idler. He's simply too lazy to be as successful as he'd like. See: LAZY, LETHARGIC, SCHLIMAZEL.

OCCUPATION: A particular course of action in which a person is habitually engaged, e.g., a job. The term comes from the Latin for "seizing, taking possession." To have a job, then, is to be possessed, as though by a demon. Yet Western civilization finds the *unoccupied* individual threatening, and wants to see him punished! Think of poor Melibeus, who, in Chaucer's *Canterbury Tales*, has "no bisynesse ne occupacion," and goes "into the fields to play"; naturally, his wife is assaulted while he's away. See: SLOTHFUL, VAGRANT.

OCCUPATIONAL THERAPY: The use of productive activity in the treatment or rehabilitation of physically or emotionally disabled people. Sounds like a job! See: LIMPSY.

OCCUPATIONALISM: A syndrome afflicting white-collar workers and tenure-track members of the professoriate. Symptoms: Disdain for amateurism; jargon. See: OTIOSE.

OLD MAN, COME THE: British slang for "shirking your duties by pretending to be old and infirm." See: MALINGERER.

OSCITANT: This term [from the Latin for "yawn"] means "drowsy," "dull," "negligent." It describes an unfortunate in a listless, enervated state. See: LANGUID, TIRED, TORPID.

OTIOSE: One of the most important pieces of information that an idler's glossary can impart is this: The Latin word for "business" is *negotium*, which means "not idling." Get it? *Otium*, or leisure, was formerly considered the true goal of life;

and business was what you were required to attend to when you weren't idling. Alas, "otiosity" now means "laziness," "ineffectuality," and "producing nothing of value." See: IDLENESS, LEISURE, WORK.

OUT-OF-WORKNESS: In his 1903 book, *The Egregious English*, Angus McNeill writes that "the English employee quirks and crawls before his employer, because he knows that his employer can exercise over him powers which, if they do not mean exactly life and death, do mean a possibly long period of out-of-workness." Some day, McNeill hopes, the Englishman will "learn that services rendered and energies expended for long periods of years without adequate reward . . . are a discredit and not an honor." See: LABOR, OTIOSE.

PASSIVE: There's a big difference between being passive [from the Latin for "acted upon"] in the sense of "not taking an active part" or being "non-cooperative," on the one hand, and in the sense of "lacking in energy or will," on the other. As we know from the phenomenon of passive resistance, sometimes not-acting can require a whole lot more energy, focus, and strength of will than acting. See: BARTLEBY, DO-NOTHING, SIT BACK.

PERAMBULATE: Although often used as a synonym for "saunter," to perambulate is to ambulate in a circle – like a workhorse, that is, or an office drone. See: AMBULATE.

PERRUQUE: French idiomatic expression describing work one does strictly for oneself while at the factory or office. In *The Practice of Everyday Life*, Michel de Certeau construes *la perruque* as a prime example of the manner in which the socio-economically weak can rip off and exploit the strong, carving out an independent domain within the oppressive circumstances imposed upon them. Maybe, maybe not. See: HOMER, DODGER.

PHILOSOPHICAL: Lin Yutang says that "philosophy began with the sense of boredom," since both involve dreaming wistfully of a better world. See: BOREDOM, DREAMER.

PISS-PUDDLE: A pejorative verb coined by a friend of the author of this glossary to describe her boyfriend's tendency to go as inert as a man lying in a puddle of his own urine when he was supposed to be making himself useful. Note that "piss about" is British slang for "waste time." See: PROCRASTINATE, UKULELE IKED.

PLAYBOY: Playboy, a turn-of-the-century descriptor for "a man who lives a life devoted to the pursuit of pleasure" has come to mean, thanks to the porn magazine, "a man who lives a life devoted to the pursuit of women with enormous breasts." See: SYBARITE.

PLOITER: Slang term meaning "to labor ineffectually." It can be applied "to amateurs and professionals alike, and to those who try hard at a given task as well as those whose hearts are just not in it," according to Peter Novobatzky and Ammon Shea's *Insulting English*. See: GOVERNMENT STROKE, HALF-ASSED.

POCOCURANTE: The Italians work hard . . . but they're under no illusion that work is the most important thing in life. Like *sprezzatura*, the term *pococurante* (nonchalance) makes slackerdom seem stylish and cool. See: INSOUCIANT, NONCHALANT, SKYLARKING.

PREOCCUPIED: "Some men are preoccupied even in their leisure: in their country house, on their couch, in the midst of solitude, even when quite alone, they are their own worst company," notes Seneca. "You could not call theirs a life of leisure." It bears repeating: To be occupied is to be possessed. See: INATTENTIVE, MINDFULNESS, OCCUPATION.

PROCRASTINATOR: Procrastination in artists "is always a symptom of an acute inner conflict," according to the literary critic Cyril Connolly. "All true artistic indolence is deeply neurotic; a pain not a pleasure." In the procrastinator [from the Latin for "put forward until tomorrow"] that lamentable failure of body and will that is languor, or torpor, becomes inextricably tangled with artistic perfectionism. It can be impossible, however – for anyone, including the procrastinator – to tell these apart. See: LANGUID, LAZY, TORPID.

PUNCTILIOCRAT: To be attentive to punctilios – the fine points, particulars, or details of conduct, ceremony, or procedure – can be a rewarding, transformative practice. Think, for example, of the *chanoyu* (Japanese tea ceremony). However, as Lao Tzu says of mere etiquette or unthinking adherence to rules of procedure, it's "the husk of all good faith." Remember that when your boss tells you to go through the proper channels. See: UPTIGHTNIK

PUT YOUR FEET UP: "How many hostesses have feared and trembled for an evening party in which the guests are not willing to loosen up," writes Lin Yutang. "I have always helped . . . by putting a leg up on top of a tea table or whatever happened to be the nearest object, and in that way forced everybody else to throw away the cloak of false dignity." See: LOLL.

QUATORZIÈME: A professional 14th guest, who can be hired on short notice by a superstitious hostess who discovers that her dinner party numbers 13. See: BON VIVANT.

QUITTER: The quitter [from the Latin for "free"] ought not to be disparaged. For as Evan Harris, author of the 1996 manual *The Quit*, informs us, quitting – a job, a bad relationship, a lifestyle – can be a creative act, a life-affirming "Yes!" See: BALK, BARTLEBY, FREE TIME.

RAMBLE: To ramble [Middle English for "roam"] means to wander for pleasure, without a fixed destination. "Got no time for spreadin' roots, the time has come to be gone," according to Led Zeppelin. "And though our health we drank a thousand times, it's time to ramble on." See: BUM, LOAF, SAUNTER.

RECALCITRANT: Etymologically, to be recalcitrant means to "kick back." Recalcitrance, then, is more than stubborn disobedience; it's a revolutionary (or at least rebellious) act of revenge. See: BALK, KICK BACK.

RECESS: Recess time at school is a mandated period of fun and physical activity designed to allow schoolchildren to blow off steam. Then they go back to work. See: VACATION.

 RECUMBENT: From the same Latin root as "incubate," which originally meant to literally "lie down on" (e.g., a hen on eggs). When you are recumbent, ideas always start hatching. See: LIE-ABED, LOLL, SUPINE.

RECUPERATE: Nietzsche writes that "More and more, work enlists all good conscience on its side; the desire for joy already calls itself a 'need to recuperate' and is beginning to be ashamed of itself." Etymologically, to recuperate is to "take back" what was stolen from you; why not stop being a victim of robbery, instead? See: FREE TIME, RELAX, VACATION.

RELAX: To relax [from the Latin for "loose," which

105

also gives us "languish" and "slack"] means to re-cuperate, i.e., from the stress of your job. We relax, that is, in order that we can return to work re-freshed. As British comedian Keith Allen says, "'relaxation' is a load of cack, it's just shit . . . I'm that relaxed all the year round, you understand?" See: FREE TIME.

ROUÉ: One who is given to, or leads, a life of plea-sure and sensuality. The name [French for "bro-ken on the wheel"] was given in the early 18th cen-tury to the rakish companions of the Duke of Orleans, to suggest that they deserved this punish-ment. See: DEBAUCHED.

SAINT-SIMONIANISM: A 19th-century socialist move-ment in France, inspired by the utopian theories of Henri de Saint-Simon, who proclaimed a brother-hood of man that must accompany the scientific organization of industry and society. Saint-Simon influenced Karl Marx, whose enthusiasm for the ennobling qualities of toil troubles idlers. See: WORKERIST.

 SANDMAN: A candy-colored clown who tiptoes to our rooms every night. See: SLEEPY.

SAUNTER: Thoreau, who wrote magnificently about the pleasures of walking aimlessly through nature, speculated that saunterers were, by virtue of their mode of ambulating, not going toward the Holy Land (*Saint Terre*); they were already in it. He wasn't far wrong, etymologically. The term actually comes from the Middle English word for "walking about musingly"; it is derived from the word "saint," as holy men were thought to spend much of their time in this manner. See: BUM, DRIFTER, FLÂNEUR, LOAF, SCAMP.

SCAMP: Like "bum" and "loaf," this obsolete verb meaning "to roam about idly" has come to be a pejorative descriptor for any footloose and fancy-free fellow. Lin Yutang, resisting the militarization of his homeland, insisted that the scamp – not the soldier – is the highest form of humanity. Whereas the latter surrenders his individuality and obeys orders, the former remains curious, dreamy, humorous, wayward, unpredictable. See: BUM, SAUNTER.

SCHLIMAZEL: A schlimazel [an Anglicization of the Yiddish compound "shemozzle" – "bad" and "luck"] is a pathetic failure, a loser who wants to succeed but cannot. See: LOSER, OBLOMOV.

SCHWEIKISM: Named after the hero of Jaroslav Hasek's comic novel, *The Good Soldier Schweik*, this is a lowbrow form of passive resistance. Employing low cunning and high spirits, a Schweikist loudly proclaims his loyalty to the prevailing authority while simultaneously defying it in a thousand small ways. See: BARTLEBY, PASSIVE, SCAMP.

SCREW THE POOCH (AND SELL THE PUPS): Early 20th-century American slang for "slack off," though with a suggestion of vile entrepreneurialism. See: GOLDBRICKER.

SCRIMSHANKER: A shirker. Military slang of obscure origin. See: SHIRKER.

SCROUNGER: From an Old English word meaning "wander about idly," a scrounger is a quick-witted type who acquires only what she needs, and only when she needs it, by foraging, scavenging, or cadging. Although it's become synonymous with sponging, scrounging is a noble art that combines – as the word itself seems to do – sauntering, lounging, and creativity. Perfect for these DIY times. See: CADGER, SAUNTER, UPCYCLE.

SEÑORITO: Once, this Spanish term referred to a carefree young bachelor, unburdened by economic responsibilities. Today, it's a pejorative applied to any male adult wealthy enough to live from capital, rents, and labor exploitation. See: SUPERFLUOUS MAN.

SHIF-MAN: Mid-20th-century West Indies slang for "ne'er-do-well," "shirker," "sluggard." Probably derived from "shiftless." See: DODGER, SLACKER.

SHIFTLESS: If shiftless ["shift" is a 16th-century English word meaning "resourcefulness"] is taken to mean "lacking in resourcefulness," then the shiftless individual is the opposite of a scrounger. See: SCROUNGER, UNAMBITIOUS.

SHIRKER: A needy, disreputable parasite, a "shark." Also: Someone who practices fraud or trickery, instead of laboring for a living; who avoids a meeting with an authority figure; who evades his duties, or obligations; who evades his work. See: DODGER, SLACKER.

SHIT-HEEL: Henry Miller writes, of young people who "know enough not to want to do a stroke of honest work," that "they prefer to be shit-heels, if they have to be. Fine! I salute them." See: CADGER.

SIESTA: This highly civilized practice of catching

forty winks during the hottest part of the day is found only in the most advanced civilizations. See: FORTY WINKS, NAP.

SINECURIST: For as long as bureaucracies have existed, there have been people eager to obtain offices and positions that require little or no work. Though a sinecure seems preferable to a job that's demanding, a sinecurist is a bird in a gilded cage: She may become too complacent to fly, even if her cage door is left open. See: DODGER, SLACKER.

 SIT BACK: "When things are going to rack and ruin," observes Henry Miller, "the most purposeful act may be to sit still." Shunryu Suzuki also values sitting. "If you sit in the right manner, with the right understanding, you attain the freedom of your being," he claims. See: DO-NOTHING, INACTION, PASSIVE.

SKIMPOLE: In Dickens's *Bleak House*, the character Skimpole says to the world: "Go your several ways in peace! Wear red coats, blue coats, lawn sleeves, put pens behind your ears, wear aprons; go after glory, holiness, commerce, trade, any object you prefer; only – let Harold Skimpole live!" Alas, though Skimpole may portray himself as one of

God's innocents, a loveable mooch, he is a monstrously selfish sponger. See: CADGER, SPONGER.

SKIVER: To "skive," a term that apparently came into English via World War I British servicemen who liked the French word *esquiver* (dodge, slink away), is to "fail to do your duty in a glorious, larger-than-life, instructive manner." Dodging is rarely as artful. See: AUTONOMISM, DODGER, FLÂNEUR, SCHWEIKISM.

SKYLARKING: "Do not take the entire world on your shoulders," Kurt Vonnegut told graduating college seniors in 1970. "Do a certain amount of skylarking, as befits people of your age. 'Skylarking,' incidentally, used to be a minor offense under Naval Regulations. What a charming crime. It means intolerable lack of seriousness. I would love to have a dishonorable discharge from the United States Navy – for skylarking not just once, but again and again and again." See: CARELESS, INSOUCIANT, POCOCURANTE.

SLACKNESS: Not to be confused with Lin Yutang's notion of "the noble art of leaving things undone," slackness [from the same Latin word for "loose" which also gives us "languish" and "relaxation"] is a blameworthy lack of due or necessary diligence, precision, or care. It's one thing to kick against the traces when odious labor is forced upon you, but an apathetic response to the prospect of any kind of sustained effort whatsoever is a different kettle of fish. Despite the Church of the Subgenius's attempt to appropriate this word for idlers, then, "slack" ought to continue being used as a synonym for "lazy." See: APATHETIC, BLASÉ, COMPLACENT, LAZY, SLACKER.

SLACKER: Unlike the idler, in whom work and leisure have combined to become something fine, the slacker remains unhappily trapped on one side of that binary opposition. Richard Linklater's movie *Slacker* may reference R.L. Stevenson's uplifting "Apology for Idlers," but Linklater admitted that the movie was a "kiss-off to a certain mindset – wallowing in negativity and being very alienated." Dr. Johnson frowned upon those so-called idlers who "boast that they do nothing, and thank their stars that they have nothing to do," and who "exist in a state of unruffled stupidity, forgetting and forgotten; who have long ceased to live." See: DODGER, LEISURE, FREE TIME, SLACKNESS.

SLACKTIVISM: A recent slang term that means "taking measures in support of a cause – signing online petitions, wearing colored bracelets, adhering bumper stickers to your car – that have little or no practical effect other than to make you feel better about yourself." Too bad that slacking is a prelude, at best, to a superior mode of existence (idling); otherwise, we'd suggest using "slacktivism" as shorthand for a revolutionary who, as Foucault put it, "wherever he finds himself, will pose the question as to whether revolution is worth the trouble, and if so which revolution and what trouble." See: BALK.

SLEEP: The periodic suspension of consciousness (during which the powers of the body are restored) that we call "sleep" ought not to be criticized in moral terms, since it's an unavoidable natural phenomenon. Sleep can, however, be criticized aesthetically, since it can be accomplished in so many different fashions, and because some people do it with so much more panache than others. See: FORTY WINKS, NAP, TIRED, DOZE.

 SLIPSHOD: Yet another curious conflation of footwear with modes of existence. How did "wearing loose shoes" come to mean "negligent"? Was Bruce Lee, in his kung fu slippers, negligent? Of course not! In honor of

Lee's philosophy, then, we should use the term slipshod to refer to a person who kicks ass without attachment to the fruits of her ass-kicking. See: FLIP-FLOP, BOOTLESS.

SLOTHFUL: Foucault claims that the practice of sentencing prisoners and madmen to forced labor arose in early modernity because of the Calvinist idea that "God helps those who help themselves." Just as homosexuality was once considered a perverse variant of the sin of willfulness, so too was sloth [from the German word that gives us "slow"] once considered an absurd variant of the sin of pride. (Absurd, so the thinking went, because the slothful person was poverty-stricken, so what did he have to be proud about?) God save us from anti-idleness fanatics! See: CALVINISM, INVISIBLE PRISON, SLUGGARD.

 SLOUCH: It seems cruel to use this term, which originally meant "drooping," and later came to mean "excessive relaxation of body muscles," to describe a lazy or incompetent person. And yet we've done so at least since 1668, when Henry More lamented the marriage of a virtuous (i.e., "upright") woman to "some poor slouching Clown." See: LOLL.

SLOW (MOVEMENT): An international grassroots effort to slow down life's pace, even to the point of turning back the clock. As chronicled in Carl Honoré's 2004 book *In Praise of Slowness*, the "slow" movement started in Italy in 1986 with slow food; it now includes slow travel, slow retail, slow neighborhoods, and slow design. NB: Like dawdling, slowing down can be a first step toward freedom, or it can be an elitist's hobby. See: DAWDLE.

SLOW-COACH: "None of your old slow-coaching days for me," insists a character in Frank E. Smedley's 1855 novel, *Harry Coverdale's Courtship*. "Life's not long enough for dreaming." An industrializing society that worships speed has no use for one who acts, works, or moves slowly. Such a person will be branded lazy – whether he actually is lazy, or instead a patient craftsman, or perhaps an idle dreamer. See: DAWDLE, SLOTHFUL.

SLUGABED: Ivan Goncharov, author of the 1859 novel *Oblomov*, is careful to show that his protagonist is not supine in the manner of a lie-abed (for whom lying down is a real sensual pleasure, and an aid to dreaming), but instead because of his lax hebetudinousness. See: EPICUREAN, LOLL, OBLOMOV.

SLUGGARD: "My indolence," lamented Dr. Johnson, "has sunk into grosser sluggishness." The sluggard [from the Norwegian word for "large heavy body," which came to mean "slow-moving person"] is a lazily inactive person, one whom lassitude has rendered tediously slow-witted and dull. See: INDOLENCE, LANGUID, LASSITUDE, TORPID.

SLUMBEROUS: To be slumberous [from the Middle English word for "doze"] is to be tired in the sense of lethargic, torpid. Slumberousness is not the same thing as indolence. See: DROWSY, LASSITUDE, LETHARGIC, TIRED, TORPID.

SNOOZE: A slang word of obscure origin. It's difficult to say, without further research, whether snoozing is more akin to dozing or napping. Are any members of the MacArthur Foundation Selection Committee reading this glossary? I hope so. See: DOZE, NAP.

SOD ABOUT: British slang for killing time. See: PISS-PUDDLE.

SPARE TIME: Time not employed or taken up by one's ordinary or usual duties or occupations. Not the same thing as free time, or leisure, then. See: FREE TIME, LEISURE.

SPLEEN: Like ennui, spleen [from the Greek word for "that internal organ believed to be the seat of moroseness, or bad temper"] is a thoroughly modern affliction, a burden borne by sophisticated urbanites incapable of resigning themselves to the subjective tyranny of (in this case) space. Sartre describes Baudelaire, whose "spleen" poems lament the sensation of being crushed under an overcast sky, or penned in by raindrops forming cell bars, as a man who suffered from a "feverish, sterile agitation, which knew that it was in vain and which was poisoned by a merciless lucidity." See: ACEDIA, ENNUI, LETHARGIC.

SPONGER: Unlike the moocher, a sort of prodigal Holy Fool to whom all right-thinking people must be generous, the sponger is a greedy, calculating parasite. Giving to the moocher can be a momentary rebellion against the project-oriented economic life; only suckers, marks, and soft touches give to a sponger. See: CADGER, SKIMPOLE.

 STARGAZER: "We are all lying in the gutter," wrote Oscar Wilde, "but some of us are looking at the stars." The stargazer is not a lazy daydreamer; instead, he is absentminded in the best possible sense. See: ABSENTMINDED, DREAMER, MINDFULNESS.

STRIKE, GENERAL: Unlike the socialist "partial strike," in which laborers participate "in readiness to resume work following external concessions and this or that modification to working conditions," noted Walter Benjamin in a 1921 essay written after a period of failed socialist uprisings in his native Germany, an anarchistic "general strike" might serve to break not only the coercive power of the state, but the stranglehold that the quotidian has on our very imaginations. See: INVISIBLE PRISON, WORKING-CLASS HERO.

STROLL: French intellectuals prefer ambulating in a manner that is purposeful but not rushed. Baudelaire, who was forced to flee his creditors by moving to Belgium, complained that "strolling, something that nations with imagination love, is not possible in Brussels." And in his philosophical travelogue, *America*, Jean Baudrillard warned of the American jogger: "Do not stop him. He will either hit you or simply carry on dancing around in front of you like a man possessed." No wonder that *le jogging* of France's America-loving president, Nicolas Sarkozy, has proven controversial. See: DRIFTER, FLÂNEUR, SAUNTER.

SUNDAY: Sartre has the protagonist of his 1938 novel, *Nausea*, observe that the carefree Sunday crowd at the seashore has "only one day in which to smooth out their wrinkles, their crow's feet, the bitter lines made by a hard week's work." See: RELAX, VACATION.

SUPERFLUOUS MAN: From Pushkin's Eugene Onegin to the protagonist of Lermontov's *A Hero of Our Time*, to Ayn Rand's *We, The Living* and Gary Shteyngart's *Absurdistan*, the Superfluous Man is an aristocratic type who can't find a place for himself in Russia's modern socio-economic system. Instead, he drinks, gambles, and womanizes. See: DALLY.

SUPINE: From the Latin for "lying on your back," the term has come to mean "inactive." But as the British artist Damien Hirst suggests with his maxim, "Minimum effort for maximum effect," there's a world of difference between idling and lazy inactivity. See: INACTIVE, LIE-ABED, LOLL, RECUMBENT, SLUGABED.

SWINGER: Once upon a time, this term [thieves' cant derived, it seems, from the Flemish word for "vagabond"] meant "rogue, rascal, scoundrel." A traveler wouldn't want to encounter the "swingeouris and scurrevagis, swankeis and swanis" mentioned by Gavin Douglas in his *Æneis* (1513).

It's a shame that in the 1960s, the term came to mean either "a lively person who keeps up with that is considered fashionable," or "a person who swaps sexual partners." Where's the frisson of danger? See: SCAMP, VAGABOND.

SYBARITE: The inhabitants of ancient Sybaris, a Greek colony in southern Italy, supposedly devoted themselves to unrestrained self-indulgence – which is how their name became synonymous with "pleasure-seeker." But unlike the Epicurean, whose quest for pleasure isn't necessarily an exhausting one, the sybarite *works* at having fun. What's the point of that? See: DEBAUCHED, DISSOLUTE, EPICUREAN, LUXURY.

THOREAUVIAN: "The mass of men lead lives of quiet desperation," according to Henry David Thoreau, the true sage of Concord. "A stereotyped but unconscious despair is concealed even under what are called the games and amusements of mankind. There is no play in them, for this comes after work." The moral of this Glossary, if any, is contained in those two sentences. See: IDLER, INVISIBLE PRISON, LABOR, LEISURE, OTIOSE.

THOUGHTLESS: Because of his absentmindedness, the idler is often accused of being thoughtless –

not in the sense of "insensitive," but in the sense of "scatterbrained." But as R.L. Stevenson makes clear, the truly thoughtless are those "dead-alive" people, engaged in a conventional occupation, who "pass those hours in a sort of coma, which are not dedicated to furious toiling in the gold-mill," and who possess "not one thought to rub against another, while they wait for the train." See: ABSENTMINDED, FORGETFUL.

TIME: In *Society of the Spectacle*, Guy Debord argues that the rich enjoy the "lazy liberty" of "historical time," in which new things can happen. The poor, however, are constrained by "cyclical" time – think of the sweep of a clock's hands – in which the same things happen over and over again. See: CLOCK, DURATION, ENNUI, KILL TIME, WORK-A-DAY.

TINKER: How did the itinerant mender of household utensils [tinker is either a contraction of "worker in tin," or an onomatopoetic word for the sound of pots being repaired] come to be synonymous with "unsuccessful mender" and "bungler"? Why are we so threatened by rootlessness? Now that hackers, makers, and crafters are cool again, perhaps the tinker – one thinks of Philip K. Dick's "variable man" – will make a comeback. See: LOAF.

TIRED: The supine idler seeks inspiration in that state of consciousness that arises between sleep and waking. The drowsy, languid slacker, however, is merely giving in to the annihilating force of torpor. See: LANGUID, LASSITUDE, RECUMBENT, RELAX, TORPID.

TORPID: Like the torpedo fish, which numbs its prey with an electric shock, "torpor" [from the Latin for "stiff," "numb"] is an enervating force which renders its victims sluggish, dull, and stagnant. See: LANGUID, LASSITUDE, LETHARGIC, SLUGGARD, TIRED.

TRAMP: The verb comes from the German word for "stamp, tread," and means "to walk with a firm, heavy, resonant step" – which sounds German, indeed. In 18th century England, a fellow who traveled from place to place on foot, in search for employment (or begging), was said to be "on the tramp," or was himself called a "tramp." See: BUM, HOBO, LOAF.

 TRUANT: R.L. Stevenson writes that "while others are filling their memory with a lumber of words, one-half of which they will forget before the week be out, your truant may learn some really useful art: to play the fiddle, to know a good cigar, or to speak with ease and opportunity to all varieties of men." See: CALVINISM, OTIOSE, SCAMP, UNEMPLOYED.

UNEMPLOYED: "I know, of course, how important it is not to keep a business engagement," remarks one of Wilde's characters, "if one wants to retain any sense of the beauty of life." To be unemployed doesn't simply mean "not engaged in a gainful occupation"; etymologically, it means "not being used." Keep that in mind! See: QUITTER.

UNAMBITIOUS, UNINDUSTRIOUS, UNPRODUCTIVE, UN-PUNCTILIOUS: Un-, un-, un-! Why aren't the words "unanal," "unuptight," and "unboring" in the dictionary? After quitting his job and moving to Paris, Henry Miller wrote *Tropic of Cancer*, a great novel that begins: "I have no money, no resources, no hopes. I am the happiest man alive." So much for the spirit of capitalism and its un-'s. See: GOOD-FOR-NOTHING, LOSER, SKIVER.

UNFREE LABOR: Work relations in which you are employed against your will (e.g., by the threat of destitution, detention, violence, or other hardship), and deprived of the right to leave, to refuse to labor, or to receive compensation in return. See: WAGE SLAVERY.

UNWORK: Capitalists and Marxists alike assume that we not only "work to live" but "live to work." That is to say, laboring, whether at a job or on our own self-development, has come to seem a kind of existential necessity. Instead of thinking of work as something that gives meaning to life, Maurice Blanchot urged us to aim for a society characterized by *desoeuvrement*, or "unworking." Unwork isn't a prescription for what to do with our free time; instead, it involves ridding oneself of those beliefs, attitudes, and material constraints that limit our freedom. See: AVOIDANCE, BALK, FREEMAN, OTIOSE.

UPCYCLE: Instead of recycling (i.e., reprocessing old materials, which is energy-inefficient), some enterprising, creative scroungers create new and useful items directly from waste materials. William McDonough and Michael Braungart, authors of *Cradle to Cradle: Remaking the Way We Make Things*, coined the term. See: SCROUNGER.

UPTIGHTNIK: Michael Cudahy, aka The Millionaire, member of the lounge-music revivalist act Combustible Edison, coined this term in his "Cocktail Nation Manifesto." The term slyly revalues all work-related values, striking back at those who'd call idlers "lazy," by informing them

(à la John Lennon) that they're crazy. See: DIS-
SOLUTE, SLUGABED.

USELESS: "There is something tragic," writes
Wilde, "about the enormous number of young
men . . . who start life with perfect profiles, and
end by adopting some useful profession." Note
also Lin Yutang's maxim that "a perfectly useless
afternoon spent in a perfectly useless manner" is
what makes life worth living. Useless actions are,
in such theories, the best way to resist the hege-
mony of a project-oriented society. See: ANA-
BHOGYA-CARYA, DETACHMENT, FIDDLE AROUND,
IDLENESS, OTIOSE.

UKULELE IKED: Before musician Cliff Edwards became the voice of Disney's Jiminy Cricket, he performed under the pseudonym Ukulele Ike. His
wistfully happy plinking can paralyze you with
emotion; this is what it means to be ukulele-iked.
See: KEF, VOLUPTÉ.

VACATION: "I think that if I had two or three
quiet days of just sheer thinking I'd upset everything," Henry Miller complained. "I ought to go
to the office one day and blow out [my boss's]
brains. That's the first step." Now you know
why your vacation [from the Latin for "free-

125

dom," ironically] is always so short, and so packed with activities: Thinking must not be permitted! See: FREE TIME, LABOR, LEISURE, OTIOSE, RECUPERATE, RELAX.

VAGABOND: In the early 15th century, a fellow having no settled means of living or no fixed home was called a "vacabond" [from the Latin for "unoccupied"]; the term was later replaced by "vagabond" [from the Latin for "wander"], which means "nomadic." The former is an itinerant laborer, the latter is footloose and fancy-free. As we learn from Roger Miller's 1965 song "King of the Road," it's possible to be both. See: BUM, HOBO.

VAGRANT: From the same Latin word that gave us "vagabond," this 15th-century legal term refers to "one of a class of persons who having no settled home or regular work wander from place to place, and maintain themselves by begging or in some other disreputable or dishonest way," according to the OED. For as long as settlements have existed, in other words, we've feared those who revert to a nomadic lifestyle. See: BUM, HOBO.

VEG (OUT): Whereas seemingly passive behavior

can sometimes be quite revolutionary, to vegetate is simply to allow oneself to become stagnant. See: CABBAGE, COUCH POTATO.

VOLUPTÉ: Aldous Huxley, noting with approval that the French are neither concerned with trying to find a metaphysical justification for the raptures of physical passion, nor propagandists of sensuality, suggests that there is no English equivalent for *volupté* [from the Latin for "pleasure."] If "voluptuousness," meaning "full of pleasure to the senses," carried the connotation of detached (but not blasé) enjoyment, we'd be close: The Epicurean seeks the detached pleasure known as *volupté*; the sybarite, voluptuousness. See: DETACHMENT, EPICUREAN, INDIFFERENT, NON-CHALANT.

 VOLUPTUARY: A voluptuary's chief interests are luxury and the gratification of his sensual appetites. He is a sybarite, not an Epicurean. See: EPICUREAN, SYBARITE.

WAGE: Compensation laborers receive in exchange for some specified quantity of their time; the word is derived from the Old French for "making a promise (in monetary form)." Not to be confused with a salary, which is paid periodically – to white-collar workers – without reference to a specified number of hours worked. "Earning a wage is a prison occupation/and a wage-earner is a sort of gaol-bird," according to D.H. Lawrence. "Earning a salary is a prison overseer's job/a gaoler instead of a gaol-bird." See: LABOR.

WAGE SLAVERY: The Lowell Mill Girls (female textile workers in Lowell, Massachusetts, in the 19th century) coined the term "wage slavery" to call attention to the similarities between buying and renting a person, and to denounce a hierarchical social order in which you are encouraged to believe that you are free to choose a job – when, in fact, your choices are severely circumscribed, and you're dependent on income derived from wage labor . . . and therefore don't have the option not to take a job. See: UNFREE LABOR.

WAITING FOR GODOT: In Beckett's little-understood play, *Waiting for Godot*, Vladimir and Estragon continue to do what they must do, even though it's frustrating and pointless, and even though no one can understand what it is they're doing – because they simply can't do anything else. The idler, whose project of self-invention and self-discovery looks to outsiders like laziness or footling, can relate. As the artist Damien Hirst says, of his own apparent inactivity: "It's like when a car is idling. You have the possibility of going somewhere, but you're not going anywhere. But that doesn't mean you're not doing anything. The energy's there." See: DO-NOTHING, GOOD-FOR-NOTHING, IDLENESS.

WASTE TIME: "There is no fun in doing nothing when you have nothing to do. Wasting time is merely an occupation then, and a most exhausting one," writes Jerome K. Jerome, in his 1886 guide-book to idleness, *The Idle Thoughts of an Idle Fellow*. See: KILL TIME.

WHILE AWAY THE HOURS: Not to be confused with killing or wasting time, to while away the hours "conferrin' with the flowers, consultin' with the rain" (as the Scarecrow sings in *The Wizard of Oz*) is a delightful variant of fiddling around. See: FIDDLE AROUND.

WORK: "Work, work, in order that by becoming poorer, you may have more reason to work and become miserable," writes Paul Lafargue. "Such is the inexorable law of capitalist production." Bertrand Russell, meanwhile, writes that it is the ruling class's "desire for comfortable idleness which is historically the source of the whole gospel of work. The last thing they have ever wished is that others should follow their [idle] example." All of which is true, but one wishes these wise men had used the term "labor," instead of "work." For as Hannah Arendt has shown us, whereas the activity of labor and the consumption of its fruits has come to dominate the public sphere, work – which is governed by human ends and intentions, and therefore exhibits a certain quality of freedom – ought to be more highly valued. See: FREE TIME, LABOR, LEISURE, IDLER, SLACKER.

WORK MAKES YOU FREE: A slogan – coined by the German nationalist author Lorenz Diefenbach in 1872, and adopted by the Nazi Party when it came to power in 1933 – posted at the entrance to a number of Nazi concentration camps. See: UNFREE LABOR.

WORK-A-DAY: According to the OED, the term means "Belonging to or characteristic of a workday or its occupations; characterized by a regular succession or round of tasks and employments; of ordinary humdrum everyday life." Work-a-day life, to paraphrase Edna St. Vincent Millay, is "one damn thing over and over." See: CLOCK, LABOR, OTIOSE, TIME.

WORK-TO-RULE: Term from the 1920s meaning "the action of strictly observing the limit's of one's occupational duties." In other words: an on-the-job strike, the unenthusiastic execution of your duties, balking that won't get you whipped. See: BALK, GOVERNMENT STROKE.

WORKAHOLIC: A 1968 coinage describing someone whose addiction to work causes him to neglect his family, withdraw from social life, and lose interest in sex. See: LISTLESS, KAROSHI.

WORKERIST: One who adopts a labor-oriented view of society. Often applied, scornfully, by laborers, to a member of the middle or upper classes who pontificates about the dignity of labor and espouses the cause of the laboring class. See: LABOR, UNWORK.

WORKERLESS: Entomological term designating social insects that have no caste system. Unfair analogies to workerless ants, who invade other ant colonies and steal their food, tend to give anarchist social theory a bad reputation. See: FREELOADER, FIDDLE AROUND.

WORKFARE: A policy of requiring welfare recipients to labor in exchange for receiving taxpayers' money. Long before the term was coined, Baudelaire mocked this brand of "compassionate conservatism" in his prose poem, "Let's Beat Up the Poor." In it, a beggar is forced to prove that he deserves charity . . . by putting up his dukes. See: UNFREE LABOR.

WORKING GIRL: US slang for "prostitute." Very telling, don't you agree? See: SKIVER, UNFREE LABOR.

WORKING-CLASS HERO: Not a hero at all, according to John Lennon's caustic 1970 song of that title. "Keep you doped with religion and sex and TV/And you think you're so clever and classless and free/But you're still fucking peasants as far as I can see." See: FREEMAN, GENERAL STRIKE, INVISIBLE PRISON.

ABOUT THE AUTHORS

Joshua Glenn is a Boston-based journalist and scholar. He has labored as a bicycle shop manager and skateboard courier, a busboy and barrel-washer, a researcher and teacher, a handyman and housepainter, a bartender and espresso jerk, and also as a magazine and newspaper editor. The only work he has ever done was: publishing Hermenaut, an intellectual zine; contributing regular columns to Feed.com, *The Idler* (UK), Britannica.com, *The London Observer*, and *The Boston Globe*'s Ideas section; and editing *Taking Things Seriously*, a 2007 collection of essays and photos devoted to oddly significant objects.

A preliminary version of this glossary appeared in *The Idler* (UK), no. 25, 1999.

After some years of graduate education in Britain and the United States, **Mark Kingwell** found he had inadvertently perfected a form of idling for which he could get paid. He is Professor of Philosophy at the University of Toronto and a contributing editor of *Harper's Magazine*, and has written for publications ranging from *Adbusters* and the *New York Times* to the *Journal of Philosophy* and *Auto Racing Digest*. Among his twelve books of political and cultural theory are the national bestsellers *Better Living* (1998), *The World We Want* (2000), and *Concrete Reveries* (2008). In order to secure financing for their continued indulgence he has also written about his various hobbies, including fishing, baseball, cocktails, and contemporary art.

ABOUT THE ILLUSTRATOR

 **Seth** is the cartoonist behind the painfully infrequent comic book series PALOOKAVILLE. His books include IT'S A GOOD LIFE IF YOU DON'T WEAKEN, WIMBLEDON GREEN, BANNOCK, BEANS AND BLACK TEA, and CLYDE FANS BOOK ONE. One volume of his sketchbooks has appeared under the title VERNACULAR DRAWINGS and another will likely appear within the following few seasons. His books have been translated into five languages.

As a book designer he has worked on a variety of projects including the recent Penguin THE PORTABLE DOROTHY PARKER. He is the designer of the 25 volume series THE COMPLETE PEANUTS and the upcoming two volume series on Canadian master cartoonist DOUG WRIGHT.

As an illustrator/hack he has produced commercial works for almost all of the major Canadian and American magazines. His work has appeared inside and on the cover of the *New Yorker*.

He lives in Guelph, Ontario with his wife and three cats and appears to rarely leave the basement.